Max Bloomfield

Bloomfield's Illustrated Historical Guide

embracing an account of the antiquities of St. Augustine, Florida - with map. To which is added a condensed guide of the St. John's, Ocklawaha, Halifax, and Indian Rivers

Max Bloomfield

Bloomfield's Illustrated Historical Guide
embracing an account of the antiquities of St. Augustine, Florida - with map. To which is added a condensed guide of the St. John's, Ocklawaha, Halifax, and Indian Rivers

ISBN/EAN: 9783337302573

Printed in Europe, USA, Canada, Australia, Japan

Cover: Foto ©Andreas Hilbeck / pixelio.de

More available books at **www.hansebooks.com**

BLOOMFIELD'S

Illustrated Historical Guide,

EMBRACING AN ACCOUNT OF THE

ANTIQUITIES OF ST. AUGUSTINE, FLORIDA

(WITH MAP).

TO WHICH IS ADDED

A Condensed Guide of the St. John's, Ocklawaha, Halifax, and Indian Rivers.

Distance Tables to Points on the above-mentioned Rivers, And Principal Cities North, East, and West.

EVERY TOURIST IN FLORIDA SHOULD PROCURE A COPY.   NO BOOK PUBLISHED CONTAINING SUCH A COMPLETE ACCOUNT.

MAX BLOOMFIELD,
BOOKSELLER, NEWSDEALER, & STATIONER,
ST. AUGUSTINE, FLA.,
EDITOR, PUBLISHER, AND PROPRIETOR.
1883.

PRICE 50 CENTS.

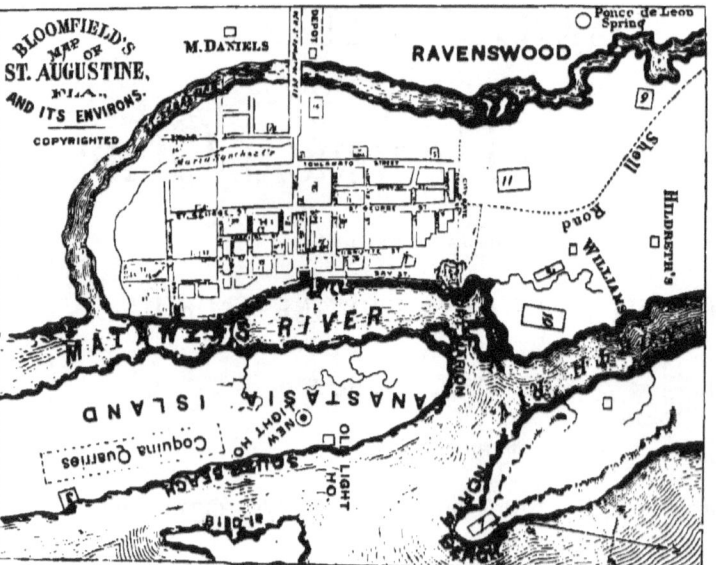

THE WHYS AND WHEREFORES.

HAVING become cognizant of the wants of the tourist, as to receiving information on all principal points of interest in the "Ancient City," we have endeavored to give as true and faithful an account as can be prepared in a condensed form.

As there are many among our visitors who would like to be informed as to the early history of St. Augustine, without going into the deep detail, which the reading of some of the works involves, we have quoted some very interesting facts from the different writers.

Included in this work we have given a complete guide to the St. John's, Ocklawaha, Halifax, and Indian Rivers, with distance table to the same, and to principal cities, north, east, and west, reckoning from Jacksonville, Florida.

Particular attention has been given to the accuracy of the appended map, which will prove an invaluable aid to all who wish to visit the different places of St. Augustine.

ST. AUGUSTINE, FLORIDA, June, 1882.

CONTENTS.

	PAGE
Whys and Wherefores,	3
St. Augustine,	7
Expeditions to Florida,	8
Huguenot Massacre,	12
St. Augustine in 1773,	15
C. B. S. on St. Augustine, 1881,	17
Spanish Governors,	18
Modern St. Augustine,	19
Public and Ancient Buildings,	21
The Spanish Cathedral,	21
Governor's Palace,	23
Oldest Houses, Spanish Corridors, etc.,	24
United States' Barracks,	26
Trinity Episcopal Church,	26
Convents,	26
The Colored Home,	27
The Plaza,	27
The Slave Market,	30
Cemeteries—Dade's Massacre—The Martyr Priest,	31
The Ancient Gateway,	37
Town Wall,	38
Fort Marion—The Escape of Wild Cat, etc.,	38
Sea Wall,	52
Anastasia Island,	52
Orange Groves, Rose Gardens, etc., etc.,	55

CONTENTS.

	PAGE
New St. Augustine,	56
Ravenswood,	56
The Yacht Club,	57
Handsome Winter Residences,	57
Bathing, Yachting, Fishing, and Hunting,	59
Country Drives,	59
Boarding-Houses,	60
History of the Minorcans,	60
St. Augustine in 1817,	69
St. Augustine in 1843—Old Customs,	73
St. Augustine During the Civil War,	79
The St. John's River,	80
Ocklawaha River,	87
Halifax and Indian Rivers,	89
Mileage on the St. John's River,	90
Mileage on the Ocklawaha River,	93
Mileage from Jacksonville to Points East, West, and North,	94
Florida Views,	95

BLOOMFIELD'S
HISTORICAL GUIDE.

ST. AUGUSTINE.

St. Augustine, Florida, is undoubtedly the oldest city, by forty years, in the United States, and was founded at a period when Spain was the greatest power on earth. Juan Ponce de Leon is supposed to have been the first one to have landed in Florida, on the Sunday before Easter, in 1512, it being Palm Sunday, which the Spaniards in those days called *Pasqua Florida*, or Flowery Easter, from the palms and roses with which the churches are decorated on that day. Therefore he gave the name of Florida to the country.

The event of founding St. Augustine did not take place till 1565, fifty-three years after the first landing of De Leon, the famous knight, who hunted for the fountain of youth. On the 8th day of May, 1565, Pedro Menendez de Aviles, at the head of some of Spain's most valiant knights, landed on the shores of Florida and planted the banner of Spain, proclaiming Philip II. the ruler of the whole continent of North America. We do not intend to go into detail, but expect to do our duty as a *Guide*, and hope to be a good and faithful one, but for the benefit of our readers we quote the following excellent article :

"EXPEDITIONS TO FLORIDA.*

" 1497. It is claimed by the English that during this year Florida was discovered by Sebastian Cabot, who did not land, but merely sailed along the East coast.

" 1512. Juan Ponce de Leon left Porto Rico in April, in continuation of his search for the Fountain of Youth, and on the second day in that month—(which day being the Sunday before Easter, is called Palm Sunday, and which the Spaniards in those days called *Pasqua Florida*, or Flowery Easter, from the palm branches and flowers with which the churches are decorated on that day)—landed on the coast, in 30 degrees and 8 minutes, north latitude, near the present site of St. Augustine, and gave the name of *Florida* to the country.

" 1516. Diego Miruelo visited the Gulf coast section and obtained pieces of gold from the Indians.

" 1517. An expedition commanded by Fernandez de Cordova visited the country.

" 1519. One Anton de Alaminos soon after visited the Gulf coast.

" 1521. Ponce de Leon made his second visit to the East coast. The Indians attacked his forces, killing great numbers. De Leon, being wounded in the conflict, was obliged to retreat to his ships. He set sail for Cuba, and soon after his arrival died from the effect of his wounds.

" 1528. Panfilo de Narvaez landed at Clear Water Bay, near Tampa. He explored the northwestern section of the State, and becoming discouraged he built several small boats and endeavored to reach Mexico. A sudden storm drove

---

* Whitney's Pathfinder.

his boat to sea, and he was never again heard of. Of the 300 who composed this expedition, only four were known to have escaped; among the number was Alvar Nunez Cabeca de Vaca, who succeeded in reaching Mexico, and from thence to Spain.

"1539. Hernando de Soto disembarked at Tampa Bay, and traversed the northwest section of the State. He continued his researches far beyond the bounds of Florida into the valley of the Mississippi, where he died, and was buried beneath its waters. The expedition then wended its way down the Mississippi River to the Gulf of Mexico, and from thence to Mexico. Of the one thousand who four years previous had landed, only three hundred reached their destination.

"1545. A treasure ship, *en route* from New Mexico to Spain, was wrecked on the eastern coast.

"1549. Four Franciscan brothers landed at Tampa Bay, and were massacred by the Indians.

"1552. About this period an entire Spanish fleet, excepting one vessel, was wrecked on the Gulf coast, while *en route* for Spain from Havana.

"1559. Don Tristan de Luna disembarked on the Gulf coast with over fifteen hundred followers, but he soon abandoned the country.

"1562. The French Protestants, or Huguenots, under Jean Ribaut, arrived on the coast, near St. Augustine. He continued north and disembarked near the mouth of St. John's River, called by the Spanish at that time St. Matheo, and erected a stone landmark, bearing the French coat of arms. Continuing north he landed at Port Royal and endeavored to established a colony. Having built Fort Charles, and leaving twenty-five men to garrison it, he returned to France. The colony, being neglected and constrained by hunger, constructed a rude vessel and set sail for their country. They succeeded in their undertaking after having experienced terrible suffering.

"1564. Rene de Laudonniere arrived at St. Augustine; continuing north he landed at St. John's Bluff, on the St. John's River, and erected Fort Caroline, where Jean Ribaut had previously erected his landmark.

"1565. August 29th, Jean Ribaut, who had previously returned to France, arrived with his colony at Fort Caroline, with supplies for Rene de Laudonniere.

"1565. Pedro Menendez de Aviles arrived on the coast and established St. Augustine, about the same time that Ribaut arrived at Fort Caroline. Menendez, upon hearing of the arrival of the French, set sail for the purpose of their extermination. He drove the French fleet from the coast and returned to St. Augustine, and immediately planned a land attack on Fort Caroline. Arriving early in the morning he attacked the fort and massacred nearly all its inmates. Laudonniere with a few others escaped. Hanging several captives to a tree, he placed above them this inscription: ' Not as Frenchmen, but as Lutherans.' On the return of Menendez to St. Augustine a solemn mass was celebrated and a Te Deum sung in commemoration of the victory. Meanwhile a severe storm overtook Jean Ribaut's fleet and all were wrecked at Matanzas, and subsequently cowardly butchered by Menendez, in squads of ten, with their hands pinioned behind their backs. Thus, in all, nearly three hundred men met their death.

"1567. Dominic de Gourgues, a Huguenot gentleman, arrived at Fort Caroline, and, with aid from the Indians, fully avenged the wickedness perpetrated by Menendez. Over the lifeless bodies of the Spanish he wrote: 'Not as unto Spaniards or outcasts, but as to traitors, robbers, and murderers.'

"1586. Sir Francis Drake made an attack on St. Augustine. He succeeded in plundering and burning the largest portion of the town. His descent resulted in the capture of £2000, which he took from the treasure-chest within the fort.

"1598. The Indians massacred several priests in and about St. Augustine.

"1665. The pirate, John Davis, made a descent upon St. Augustine and pillaged the town.

"1702. Governor Moore, of South Caroline, captured St. Augustine, and held the town for three months; before he withdrew he burned it. He, however, failed to capture the fort.

"1740. General Oglethorpe laid siege to the town. He planted his guns on Anastasia Island, also behind the sand-hills on Point Quartell. He also erected a sand battery on Anastasia Island, opposite the fort. After an unsuccessful attempt of forty days to capture the fort, he withdrew. He again in 1743 marched to the very gates of St. Augustine, but met with no better success.

"1763. Spain ceded Florida to Great Britain.

"1766. It was receded to Spain.

"1819. Florida passed into the hands of the United States. The change of flags occurred in East Florida, at St. Augustine, July 10th, 1821.

"1845. Florida was admitted into the Union as a State."

This article will give the reader a very fair idea how eventful must have been the early history of St. Augustine.

The old saying, "If walls could speak," does not come amiss here, for they undoubtedly could tell tales far more thrilling than the most absorbing of our melodramatic tales in fiction.

HUGUENOT MASSACRE.

For the benefit of our readers we will give the translation of the account of the Huguenot massacre, being a memorandum of a letter by the chaplain of the expedition under Menendez:

"Your Excellency will remember that when I was in Spain I went to see the General at the Port St. Marie, and that he showed me a letter from monseigneur the King, Don Philip, signed by his hand, in which his majesty stated, that on the 20th of May, the same year, seven French ships, bearing seven hundred men and two hundred women, had sailed for Florida."

(Then follows a description of the armament of the Spanish fleet, and the instructions given to the Adelantado, Pedro Menendez, to proceed to Florida and claim the country for the King of Spain.—*Translator.*)

"On the eighth of the month, the day of the nativity of Our Lady, the General landed, with many banners displayed, to the sound of trumpets and of other instruments of war, and amid salvos of artillery. I took a cross and went before them chanting *Te Deum Laudamus*. The General marched straight to the cross, followed by all those who accompanied him; they knelt and kissed the cross. A great many Indians witnessed the ceremonies, and imitated all that they saw done. The same day the General took possession of the country in the name of His Majesty. All the captains swore allegiance to him as their General, and as Adelantado of the country.

* * * * * *

"We are in this fort to the number of six hundred combatants.

* * * * * *

"To-day as I finished the mass of Our Lady, the Admiral was informed that a Frenchman had been captured. He told us that our enemies had embarked more than two hundred men on four vessels to go in search of our fleet; God our Father sent suddenly so great a tempest that these men must have been destroyed, for since their departure, have occurred the worst tempests I ever saw. The following Monday we saw a man approach, who cried out loudly: 'Victory! victory! the French fort is in our hands.' I have already stated that the enterprise which we have undertaken is for the glory of Jesus Christ and of His Mother. The Holy Spirit has enlightened the reason of our chief, in order that all may be turned to our profit, and that we might gain so great a victory. The enemy did not perceive them until they were attacked, most of them being in bed; many arose in their night-clothes, and begged for quarter. Notwithstanding this, one hundred and forty-two were killed, the rest escaped. In an hour's time the fort was in our possession.*

"A few days after this some Indians came to our fort and informed us, by signs, that a French vessel had been wrecked

---

* Fort Caroline.

on Anastasia Island.* The General, with the Admiral and many followers, repaired to the coast, and taking with him a Frenchman, who had accompanied us from Spain, he called to them to come over. A French gentleman, who was a sergeant, brought their reply to the summons to surrender; for they had raised a flag as a signal of war. He said that they would surrender on condition that their lives might be spared. The General demanded an unconditional surrender. Seeing that no other resource remained to them, in a short time they all surrendered themselves to his discretion.

"Seeing that they were Lutherans, his Excellency condemned them all to death; but, as I was a priest and felt a sympathy for them, I begged him to grant me a favor,—that of sparing those who would embrace our holy faith. He granted me this favor. I succeeded in thus saving ten or twelve; all the rest were executed because they were Lutherans and enemies of our holy Catholic faith. All this took place on the day of St. Michael, September 22d, 1565. There were one hundred and eleven Lutherans executed, without counting fourteen or fifteen prisoners."

Francisco Lopez de Mendoza Grajales, Chaplain of his Excellency, certify that the foregoing is true.
    Francisco Lopez de Mendoza Grajales.

A Huguenot survivor of the attack on Fort Caroline has described that human butchery as "a massacre of men, women, and little infants, so horrible that one can imagine nothing more barbarous and cruel."

---

* Directly opposite where Fort Matanzas now stands.

ST. AUGUSTINE IN 1773.

St. Augustine has changed remarkably in the last few years. A great many old landmarks are continually being removed to make way for enterprises of various kinds. To give the reader an idea of St. Augustine, many years ago, we will quote Stork's description of it as it appeared about 1773:

"The town of St. Augustine is situated near the glacis of the fort, on the west side of the harbor. It is an oblong square. The streets are regularly laid out, and intersect each other at right angles. They are built narrow on purpose to afford shade. The town is above half a mile in length, regularly fortified with bastions, half bastions, and a ditch. Besides these works, it has another sort of fortification, very singular, but well adapted against the Indians, an enemy the Spaniards had most to fear. It consists of several rows of palmetto trees, planted very close along the ditch, up to the parapet. Their pointed leaves are so many chevaux-de-frise, that make it entirely impenetrable. The two southern bastions are built of stone.

"In the middle of the town is a spacious square, called the Parade, open towards the harbor. At the bottom of this square is the governor's house, the apartments of which are spacious and suited to the climate, with high windows, a balcony in front, and galleries on both sides. To the backpart of the house is joined a tower, called in America a lookout, from which there is an extensive prospect, towards the sea as well as inland. There are two churches within the walls of the town, the Parish Church, a plain building, and another belonging to the Convent of Franciscan Friars, which is converted into barracks for the garrison. The houses are built of freestone, commonly two stories high, two rooms upon a floor, with large windows and balconies. Before the entry of most of the houses runs a portico of stone arches. The roofs are commonly flat. The Spaniards consulted convenience more than taste in their buildings. The number of houses in the town and within the lines when the Spaniards left it was above 900; many of them, especially in the suburbs, being built of wood, are now gone to decay.

"The inhabitants, of all colors, whites, negroes, mulattoes, Indians, etc., at the evacuation of St. Augustine, amounted to 5700, including the garrison of 2500 men. Half a mile from the town, to the west, is a line, with a broad ditch and bastions, running from St. Sebastian's Creek to St. Mark's River. A mile further is another fortified line, with some redoubts, forming a second communication between a stoccata fort, upon St. Sebastian's River, and Fort Mosa, upon the river St. Mark's.

"Within the first line, near the town, was a small settlement of Germans, who had a church of their own. Upon St. Mark's River, within the same line, was also an Indian town, with a church built of freestone. What is very remarkable, the steeple is of good workmanship and taste, though formerly built by the Indians. The governor has given the lands belonging to this township as glebe-lands to the Parish Church."

St. Augustine in 1882 is undoubtedly a beautiful spot, but, by what we glean from old writers, in ancient times it must have presented a scene of great beauty, with its profusion of orange groves and lovely flower gardens.

In January, 1766, the thermometer sank to 26° above zero. The only snow-storm remembered was during the winter of 1774; the inhabitants spoke and thought of it as the "white rain." But the coldest weather ever known in Florida or St. Augustine was in February, 1835, when the thermometer sank to 7° above zero, and the St. John's River froze several rods from the shore. This freeze proved a great injury to St. Augustine, for it killed every fruit tree in the city, and deprived the majority of the people of their only income. The older inhabitants still remark, that the freeze of 1835 cost most of them their all.

"C. B. S." on St. Augustine in 1881.

This is how it strikes " C. B. S.," of *Winter Cities in Summer Land:*

"Then morning comes, 'and such a morning as does not come anywhere except at St. Augustine;' and the verdict, St. Augustine is *not* what all the other world is, is the universal one. And then with wanderings through the quaint old streets, sailing down the bay to the light-houses and the coquina quarries, gathering shells by the seashore, quiet strolls along the Sea-wall, resting now under the shadow of the watch-tower in the Castle San Marco, the hours fly so quickly, but not too quickly, to paint the pictures that memory loves to call her own."

For the benefit of our readers we will enumerate the names of those who have ruled St. Augustine, until the change of flags.

SPANISH GOVERNORS *

1. Juan Ponce de Leon, landed 1512
2. Lucas Vasquez de Ayllon, ... 1524
3. Panfilo de Narvaez, ... 1527
4. Hernando de Soto, appointed 1537, died . . 1542
5. Tristan de Luna, ... 1559-61
6. Angel de Villafane, ... 1561
7. Pedro Menendez de Aviles, . . . 1565-72
8. Pedro Menendez Marquez, killed . . . 1574
9. Hernando de Miranda, ... 1575-93
10. John D. Salinas, ... 1593-1619
11. Diego de Rebolledo, ... 1655
12. Juan de Hita y Salazar, ... 1676-79
13. Pablo de Hita, commenced 1679
14. John Marquez Cabrera, in 1680
15. Francesco de la Guerra, commenced . . 1684
16. Diego de Quiroga, ... 1690
17. Laureano de Torrez i Ayala, in . . 1693
18. Joseph de Zuñiga i la Cerda, till . . 1708
19. Francesco de Corcoles Martinez, Captain-General, 1708-12
20. Juan de Ayala y Escobar, commenced . . 1712
21. Anthony Benavides, ... 1719-30
22. Francesco de Moral Sanchez, . . . 1730-37
23. Manuel de Montiano, ... 1737-41
24. Alonso Hernandez de Herida, . . . 1755-58
25. Lucas Fernando Palacios, ... 1758-62

The above still lacks about ten names of being complete. The following were the Captains-General during the second Spanish supremacy:

1. Vincente Manuel de Zespedez, . . . 1784
2. José de Galvez, ... 1786
3. Juan Nepomuceno Quesada, ... 1790
4. Enrique White, ... 1796
5. Juan José de Estrada, ... 1811
6. Sebastian Kindalem, ... 1812
7. Juan José de Estrada (second term), . . 1815
8. José Coppinger, ... 1816-21

* Whitney's Pathfinder.

We have given the reader such portions of history as will serve to familiarize him with the early days of St. Augustine. We will now attend to our real object,—a faithful guide.

MODERN ST. AUGUSTINE.

St. Augustine is now chiefly an attractive and delightful winter resort, and, on account of its historical relations, is undoubtedly the resort to which the tourist or invalid is most partial. It is situated about thirty-five miles from Jacksonville, directly south, and fifteen miles from the St. John's River, east.

It is on a peninsula, bounded on the north by the mainland, on the east by North River, the harbor channel and the Matanzas River separating it from Anastasia Island, on the ocean; and on the south and west by the San Sebastian River. The city occupies the same point upon which Menendez first located, who gave the name of St. Augustine to the town, as he arrived on the coast on the day dedicated to that Saint. It having previously been an Indian village, by the name of Selooe or Seloy, for the Spanish found habitations in considerable numbers.

In addition to the Catholic Cathedral, the city possesses six churches; Presbyterian (1), Episcopalian (1), Methodist (colored 1), Baptist (colored 2), and African (1). Four excellent schools are at all times well attended. 1st. Peabody Fund School, No. 1. 2d. Peabody Fund School, No. 2, for colored children. 3d. The Convent School, for girls, where excellent tuition is given by the "Sisters of St. Joseph." 4th. The Sisters' School, for boys. For a general education the Peabody School will compare favorably with any in the country; and parents desiring to remain here during the winter can with safety allow their children to attend.

The ancient city has two newspapers, both weekly. The *St. John's Weekly*, M. R. Cooper, Esq., editor, issued every Friday evening.

The *St. Augustine Press*, J. F. Whitney, Esq., editor, issued every Thursday evening.

From January to May we have two mails daily, and your newspaper is but thirty-six hours old on its arrival from New York, Philadelphia, Boston, Chicago, Cincinnati, etc.

Communication by telegraph is unsurpassed, and the express companies' service is daily.

The hotel and boarding-house accommodations are ample, and better than ever. St. Augustine is especially beneficial to invalids for its excellent sea-bathing, which can be enjoyed at the bath-house, either hot or cold. Another great feature is the artesian well, the mineral qualities of which is said to be equal to that of Saratoga, Bedford, and other famous springs.

We will now enter the quaint old town and take a look at all there is to be seen. The first thing that will strike you as being peculiar is the streets, of which there are a number. The principal ones run north and south. Bay Street, the widest of all, faces the water; the next, west of this, is Charlotte Street; next is St. George, then comes Tolomato Street. Hospital Street also runs north and south, commencing at King Street, and running to Bridge Street; the latter runs east and west. King Street is the principal one running east and west; it begins at the depot and ends at the Seawall. You will be greatly attracted as you pass through this street by the lovely lane with its overhanging trees of oak and pride of India. The narrowest street in the city is Treasury, portions of which are only seven feet wide, and you can with very little exertion shake hands across it. The narrowness of the streets and the hanging balconies add greatly to the quaintness of the whole. The old houses, generally built close to the street, are apt to give the exterior a barren look; if the visitor will take the trouble to give a peep into the court or rear yard, he will be astonished to see the semi-tropical scene that presents itself. The streets in the old Spanish times were floored with concrete, and vehicles and horses were not allowed to travel on them.

The Shell Road, formerly called King's Road, leading from the City Gates to Jacksonville, was constructed in 1765, by subscription; 'tis the favorite drive in the city, and leads to "Magnolia Grove," about five miles out, noted for the grand avenues of live oaks, which are profusely draped with Spanish moss. 'Tis a place well worth visiting.

The old Spanish residences are constructed of coquina, a conglomeration of shell and sand, the quarries of which are situated on Anastasia Island. 'Tis said that the old-time Spanish houses were flat-roofed.

PUBLIC AND ANCIENT BUILDINGS.

The Spanish Cathedral.—This is undoubtedly the quaintest-looking structure in the city. It was completed in 1793, at a cost of over $16,000. Its quaint Moorish belfry, with four bells, which are set within separate niches, together with the clock forms a complete cross.

22   BLOOMFIELD'S HISTORICAL GUIDE.

Upon one of the bells appears the following:

SANCTE JOSEPH
ORA PRO NOBIS
D 1682

This bell was probably taken from the ruins of a previous church, located on the west side of St. George Street. The other bells have inscriptions on them, but no date. The small bell in the upper niche was placed there about fifty years ago, having been presented to the church by Don

FIG. 1.

THE SPANISH CATHEDRAL AT ST. AUGUSTINE, FLORIDA.

Geronimo Alverez. The ceiling of the church is painted; the floor, now of wood, was formerly concrete. There is one painting of interest hanging on its walls, bearing the following inscription:

ST. AUGUSTINE.

FIRST MASS IN SAINT AUGUSTINE, FLORIDA, SEP. 8, 1565, AT THE LANDING OF THE SPANIARDS UNDER PEDRO MENENDEZ.
WITH RELIGION CAME TO OUR SHORES CIVILIZATION, ARTS, SCIENCES AND INDUSTRY.

This painting is supposed to be not the imagination of some person, but a *true* copy of the landing of the Spanish as inscribed on the picture. Near the altar hangs a unique lamp of solid silver, in which has been kept burning the sacred flame, almost without intermission, for nearly a hundred years. Near the vestibule, upon the left as you enter the church, is the sacred crucifix belonging to the early chapel of Nra Sra de la Leche. It is said that another ornament of this chapel, a statue representing the Blessed Virgin watching from the church over the camp of the new believers in her Son's divinity, is in the convent of St. Theresa, at Havana. A very interesting document is probably in the possession of the church in Cuba, which is an inventory taken under a decree, issued February 6th, 1764, by Morel, Bishop of Santa Cruz, enumerating all the ornaments, altars, effigies, bells, and jewels, belonging to the churches and religious associations of St. Augustine. This inventory, and much of the property, was taken to Cuba in a schooner, called *Our Lady of the Light*. From this record it might be possible to learn something of the history of the bells in the belfry.*

GOVERNOR'S PALACE,

Now used as the Post-Office, Custom House, and Public Library, stands directly opposite the western side of the

---

* Dewhurst's History of St. Augustine, published in 1881.

Plaza, corner of St. George and King streets. Under the skill of modern workmanship it has lost its quaint appearance, for it truly was a quaint-looking structure, with its lookout towers and balconies, and the handsome gateway, mentioned by De Brahm, which is said to have been a fine specimen of Doric architecture. It was completely surrounded by a thick coquina wall, the remains of which can still be seen on the northern side of the building; the corners of this wall rose up in columns about eight feet higher than the wall. One of these columns is still standing, in excellent preservation, looming grimly up next door to Bloomfield's Stationery Emporium.

OLDEST HOUSES, SPANISH CORRIDORS, ETC.

St. Augustine has a great many old houses. Each history and guide picks out some other structure to be its "oldest house" in town, therefore, we will try to enumerate them all, and then "you pays your money and takes your choice."

The wall opposite the United States Barracks, upon which reclines the "Date-Palm" tree, is said to be the oldest wall in the city; this is very probable, as we have heard it remarked by one of our old Spanish Dons, aged seventy-eight years, that he remembers that both wall and tree stood there when he was a child.

Brinton, in his *Guide to Florida* (1869), says: "The 'oldest house' in town is at the corner of Green Lane and Bay Street. A century ago it was the residence of the English Attorney-General, and probably was built about 1750. The house decayed for want of occupancy, and the wood, being a sort of royal palm, fell a prey to the relic-hunting tourist and the curiosity dealers, who made walking-canes from it." On Hospital Street, between Artillery and Green Lane, stands a very old coquina building, used now as a

Fig. 2.

ST. FRANCIS STREET OPPOSITE UNITED STATES BARRACKS.

storehouse, the rear of which presents a good idea of a Spanish house, showing the characteristic Spanish corridors. This is undoubtedly a very old house. But the oldest original walls now standing in the United States, are the

UNITED STATES BARRACKS.

This building was once used and designated as the "St. Francis Convent," the appearance of which has been much changed by the extensive repairs and alterations made by the United States government. It had formerly a large circular lookout upon the top, from which a beautiful view of the surrounding country was obtained. The building is located at the south end of the town, at the terminus of the Sea-wall, and occupied at present by United States troops. Concerts are given by the military band, in the parade ground fronting the barracks, twice a week. Guard mount, a very interesting sight, in which the band participates, can be witnessed every morning, Sundays included, at 9 o'clock.

TRINITY EPISCOPAL CHURCH,

Standing on the southern side of the Plaza, directly opposite the Spanish Cathedral, was commenced in 1827, and consecrated in 1833, by Bishop Bowen, of South Carolina.

THE PRESBYTERIAN CHURCH

Was built about 1830. It is a plain coquina building, situated on St. George Street, between Bridge and St. Francis streets.

CONVENTS.

The *old* convents are all of the past. The very old convent of St. Mary was situated on the site just opposite the Bishop's residence. In the rear of Bloomfield's News Emporium stands what was formerly the new St. Mary's Convent, but the same is vacant now, the lower floors only being used for school purposes. The Convent of the Sisters of St. Joseph is a fine coquina building, located on St. George Street, about one block south of the Plaza. A visit to the same is quite interesting. A particularly fine display of laces, and Spanish and Mexican work, can here be seen.

THE COLORED HOME

For the aged is located on Bronson Street, near King, and close to the Maria Sanchez Creek. It is a large two-and-one-half story building, with mansard roof, and has broad piazzas. The Home was endowed by Buckingham Smith, Esq., and built by the late Dr. Isaac Bronson.

THE PLAZA.

What would St. Augustine be without its Plaza? Thanks to Holmes Ammidown, Esq., it is now an object of pride. Previous to his good work, it was the resort of stray horses and cattle. 'Tis here that the balmy sea-breeze can always be enjoyed beneath the shade of the pride of India, or the sturdy oak. Not alone for its natural beauties should it be treasured, but also for its historical connections. "The Plaza de la Constitucion," is situated in the centre of the city. During the early part of the Revolution, effigies of John Hancock and Samuel Adams were burned here by the British troops. Nearly in the centre of the square stands a monument, twenty feet high, erected in 1812, in commemoration of the "Spanish Liberal Constitution." A short time after, the government gave orders that it should be torn down. The citizens of St. Augustine, upon hearing of this order, quietly removed and concealed the inscribed marble tablets. The monument remained undisturbed. In

1818 the tablets were quietly replaced. Of the monuments erected in commemoration of the Constitution, this is the only one now standing. Upon the east side is the larger marble tablet, upon which is engraved the following:

    Plaza de la
    Constitucion.
  Promulga en esta Ciudad
  de San Agustin de la Florida
  Oriental en 17 de Octubre de
  1812 siendo Gobernador el
   Brigadier Don Sebastian
    Kindalem Cuba Hero
   del order de Santiago
   Peira eterna memoria
  El Ayuntamiento Consti-
  tucional Erigioeste Obelisco
  dirigido por Don Fer-
   nando de la Plaza
   Arredondo el Joven
   Regidor De cano y
  Don Francisco Robira
   Procurador Sindico.
    Año de 1813.

TRANSLATION.

 Plaza of the Constitution, promulgated in the city of St. Augustine, East Florida, on the 17th day of October, the year 1812. Being then Governor the Brigadier Don Sebastian Kindalem, Knight of the Order of San Diego.

FOR ETERNAL REMEMBRANCE,

the Constitutional City Council erected this monument under the supervision of Don Fernando de la Maza Arredondo, the young municipal officer, oldest member of the corporation, and Don Francisco Robira, Attorney and Recorder.

"Immediately under the date there is cut in the marble tablet, the Masonic emblem of the square and compass.

The reader can readily believe that the City Council of St. Augustine, in 1813, were all too good Catholics to be responsible for this symbol of Masonry. The history of that piece of vandalism is said to be as follows: Soon after the close of the war of the rebellion, the 'young bloods' amused themselves by endeavoring to create an alarm in the mind of the United States commandant, and by executing a series of cabalistic marks at different localities throughout the town, to convey the impression that a secret society was in existence, and about to do some act contrary to the peace and dignity of the United States. Besides other marks and notices posted upon private and public buildings about the town, this square and compass was one night cut upon the tablet of the Spanish monument, where it will remain as long as the tablet exists, an anomaly without this explanation."*

Opposite the Spanish monument stands the Confederate one, erected in 1880, by the "Ladies Memorial Society," in memory of the soldiers of St. Augustine, who fell in the late war, the names of whom are inscribed on the large tablets. The following inscriptions are on the smaller slabs on the east and west sides.

OUR DEAD.

Erected by the Ladies' Memorial Association, of St. Augustine, Florida, A.D. 1872.†

IN MEMORIAM.

Our loved ones, who gave their lives in the service of the Confederate States.

---

* Dewhurst's History of St. Augustine, 1881.

† The first monument was erected in 1872. It was in the shape of a broken shaft on a pillar or pedestal. It stood on St. George Street almost diagonally opposite the Presbyterian church.

30   BLOOMFIELD'S HISTORICAL GUIDE.

The following inscription is on the south side:

>They died far from the home that gave them birth.
>By comrades honored, and by comrades mourned.

On the north side:

>They have crossed the river and rest under the shade of the trees.

THE SLAVE MARKET.

East of the Confederate monument stands the old, old market. A queer-looking structure it is. 'Tis hard to name its style of architecture, therefore we will call it a piece of

FIG. 3.

THE OLD SLAVE MARKET AT ST. AUGUSTINE, FLORIDA.

Augustinian mechanism. Four years ago it was used as a meat market, but since, the Council and a private gentleman have rescued it from what must have been degrading to this proud piece of Spanish antiquity, of which very little is known. We have been told that before the war it was used as a *slave market*. Whenever a *sale* was to take place the bell in the cupola would be rung to notify the public. The reader will please understand that the compiler of this Guide does not hold himself responsible for the slave-market story, but, in the words of the *old sergeant* at the fort, will say : " I'm only giving it to ye as it was given to me, d'ye moind now ?"

Situated in the Plaza will be found the artesian well, of the mineral qualities of which we have already spoken.

CEMETERIES—DADE MASSACRE, ETC.

We will now take the interested stranger to the military burying-ground, which is located just south of the United States Barracks. Under three pyramids here are interred the remains of Major Dade and his one hundred and seven comrades, who were massacred by the Indians when on their way to the Withlacoochee River to join General Clinch. These were sent from Fort Brooke, at Tampa, to reinforce General Clinch, and on the 28th of December, 1835, were attacked by eight hundred Indians in ambush. At the first fire more than half the soldiers were killed or wounded, but the remainder returned the fire, and a small six-pounder cannon was used with some effect until the artillerymen were all killed or wounded. The Indians then showed themselves, leaving their ambush and thus disclosing their numbers, of whom one hundred were mounted. The fight was kept up for an hour, when the Indians slackened their fire, and the soldiers felled trees and erected a triangular fortress as a protection. The respite, however, was temporary. The Indians again rushed on with whoop and yell to complete the fearful butchery, and a desperate hand to hand conflict was maintained, until all but three of the soldiers were killed or wounded. These three managed to escape and tell the sad tale. During the conflict the soldiers used their bayonets and clubbed their muskets, and the Indians made use of their knives and tomahawks.

After the battle the wounded were killed and scalped, and the victors danced a war dance over the battle-ground, and at length left the field of carnage with the dead unburied, lying in the postures in which they had fallen.

A dog belonging to Captain Gardner escaped and returned to Tampa, giving at that place the first intimation of the bloody work that had been perpetrated. When fresh troops arrived on the scene, they beheld their dead comrades lying where they had fallen, with the stern expression of battle still on their faces, which were turned in the direction of the quarter from which their savage foes had attacked them. They were buried on the battle-field, and the sixpounder cannon was placed upright in the ground to mark the spot. Their remains were afterwards removed to this place.

In the old Spanish graveyard, situated on Tolomato Street, just north of the Ball orange grove, you will find some very queer and antique-looking tombs. It is forbidden by the city to bury any one in this old cemetery unless the parties have a vault. This cemetery is one of the most historic spots in or about St. Augustine.

"In 1592 twelve Franciscan missionaries arrived at St. Augustine, with their Superior, Fray Jean de Silva, and placed themselves under the charge of Father Francis Manon, Warden of the Convent of St. Helena. One of these, a Mexican, Father Francis Panja, drew up in the language of the Yemassees his abridgment of *Christian Doctrine*, said to be the first work compiled in any of our Indian languages.

"The Franciscan Father Corpa established a mission home for the Indians at Tolomato, in the northwest portion of the city of St. Augustine, where there was an Indian village. Father Blas de Rodriques, also called Montes, had an Indian church at the village of the Indians called Tapoqui, situated on the creek called Cano de la Leche, north of the fort. Upon this site is now the new Catholic cemetery. It is just outside of the City Gates, and is reached by way of the Shell Road. The walls of the chapel are modern. The same was destroyed a few years ago by a severe northeaster, and the church, bearing the name of 'Our Lady of the Milk,' was situated on the elevated ground, a quarter of a mile north of the fort, near the creek. A stone church existed at this locality as late as 1795, and the crucifix belonging to it is preserved in the Roman Catholic church at St. Augustine. These missions apparently were attended with considerable success, large numbers of the Indians being received and instructed both at this and other missions.

"Among the converts at the mission of Tolomato was the son of the Cacique, of the province of Guale, a proud and high-spirited young leader, who by no means submitted to the requirements of his spiritual father, but indulged in excesses which scandalized his profession. Father Corpa, after trying private remonstrances and warnings in vain, thought it necessary to administer to him a public rebuke. This aroused the pride of the young chief, and he suddenly left the mission, determined upon revenge. He gathered from the interior a band of warriors, whom he inspired with his own hatred against the missionaries. Returning to Tolomato with his followers, under cover of the night, he crept up to the mission house, burst open the chapel doors, slew the devoted Father Corpa while at prayers, then severed his head from his body, set it upon a pike-staff, and threw his body out into the forest, where it could never afterwards be found. The scene of this tragedy was in the neighborhood of the present Roman Catholic cemetery of St. Augustine.

"As soon as this occurrence became known in the Indian village all was excitement, some of the most devoted bewailing the death of their spiritual father, while others dreaded the consequences of so rash an act, and shrank with terror from the vengeance of the Spaniards, which they foresaw would soon follow. The young chief of Gaule gathered them around him, and in earnest tones addressed them. 'Yes,' said he, 'the Friar is dead. It would not have been had he allowed us to live as we did before we became Christians. We desire to return to our ancient customs, and we must provide for our defence against the punishment which will be hurled upon us by the governor of Florida, which, if it be allowed to reach us, will be as rigorous for this single friar as if we killed them all. For the same power which we possess to destroy one priest we have to destroy them all.' His followers approved of what had been done, and said there was no doubt but what the same vengeance would fall upon them for the death of one as for all. He then resumed: 'Since we shall receive equal punishment for the death of this one as though we had killed them all, let us regain the liberty of which these Friars have robbed us, with their promises of good things, which we have not yet seen, but which they seek to keep us in hope of while they accumulate on us, who are called Christians, injuries and disgust, making us quit our wives, restricting us to one only, and prohibiting us from changing her. They prevent us from having our balls, banquets, feast celebrations, games, and contests, so that being deprived of them we lose our ancient valor and skill, which we inherited from our ancestors. Although they oppress us with labor, refusing to grant even a respite of a few days, and although we are disposed to do all they require from us, they are not satisfied; but for everything they reprimand us, injuriously treat us, oppress us, lecture us, call us bad Christians, and deprive us of all the pleasures, the which our fathers enjoyed, in the hope that they would give us heaven, by their subjecting us and holding us under their absolute control; and what have we to hope except to be made slaves? If we now put them all to death, we shall destroy these excrescences, and force the governor to treat us well.' The majority were carried away by this address, and rang out the war-cry of death and defiance. While still eager for blood their chief led them to the Indian town of Tapoqui, the mission of Father Montes, on Cano de la Leche. Tumultuously rushing in they informed the missionary of the fate of Father Corpa, and that they sought his own life and those of all his order, and then with uplifted weapons bade him prepare to die. He reasoned and remonstrated with them, portraying the folly and wickedness of their intentions; that the vengeance of the Spaniards would surely overtake them, and implored them with tears that for their own sake rather than his they would pause in their mad designs. But all in vain. They were alike insensible to his eloquence and his tears, and pressed forward to surround him. Finding all else in vain, he begged as a last favor that he should be permitted to celebrate mass before he died. In this he was probably actuated in part by the hope that their fierce hatred might be assuaged by

the sight of the ceremonies of their faith, or that the delay
might afford time for succor from the adjoining garrison
The permission was given, and then for the last time the
worthy Father put on his robes of sacrifice. The wild and
savage crowd, thirsting for his blood, reclined upon the floor
and looked on in sullen silence, awaiting the conclusion of
the rites. The priest alone, standing before the altar, proceeded with this most sad and solemn mass, then cast his
eyes to heaven and knelt in private supplication, when the
next moment he fell under the blows of his most cruel foes,
bespattering the altar, at which he ministered, with his own
life's blood. His crushed remains were thrown into the
fields, that they might serve for the fowls of the air or the
beasts of the forest, but not one would approach it except a
dog, which, rushing forward to lay hold of the body, fell
dead upon the spot, says the ancient chronicle, and an old
Christian Indian, recognizing it, gave it sepulture in the
forest. From thence the ferocious young chief of Gaule led
his followers against several other missions in other parts
of the country, which he attacked and destroyed, together
with the attendant clergy. Thus upon the soil of the ancient
city was shed the blood of Christian martyrs, who were
laboring with a zeal well worthy of emulation, to carry the
truths of religion to the native tribes of Florida. Two hundred and fifty years have passed since these scenes were
enacted, but we cannot even now repress a tear of sympathy
and a feeling of admiration for those self-denying missionaries of the cross, who sealed their fate with their blood,
and fell victims to their energy and devotion. The specta-
cle of the dying priest, struck down at the altar, attired in
his sacred vestments and perhaps imploring pardon upon

his murderers, cannot fail to call up in the hearts of the most insensible something more than a passing emotion."*

The Huguenot Cemetery is located just outside the City Gates, and *on the west side of the Shell Road.*

THE ANCIENT GATEWAY,

Commonly called the City Gates, is located directly north of St. George Street, and west of Fort Marion, being almost parallel with the fort. It is flanked by two square pillars with Moorish tops. On each side a dry ditch

FIG. 4.

THE OLD CITY GATE AT ST. AUGUSTINE, FLORIDA.

and the remains of a wall. It is a picturesque and imposing structure. The supposition is that a wall extended around the whole city, but it is doubtful; 'tis more likely that Orange Street may have been barricaded by logs and earth; nevertheless, we will quote what the *Whitney Pathfinder* thinks about the

---

* Fairbanks's History and Antiquities of St. Augustine.

TOWN WALL.

Whether this wall was composed of the same material as the old fort, or was merely a rough stockade of pine logs, is a matter of conjecture. If a stone wall ever existed, it probably now forms a part of some of the old structures in the city. However, this wall or stockade is supposed to have been built some two hundred years ago. The north end portion of this wall was situated on the south bank of the ditch, and extended west to the St. Sebastian River, where it ended in a bastion, of which at present time, with the exception of the sand elevation, no trace remains.

The ditch, at the present day, is quite visible, and at one time it connected the moat-water around the fort with the St. Sebastian River; but during the late war all evidence of this connection was destroyed by the construction of the northwest fort embankment.

In 1871, there existed on the corner of Tolomato and King Streets, a lunette, constructed of coquina stone, from twelve to fifteen feet high, and though it was to visitors an object of attraction nearly equal to that of the City Gates, it was removed for personal benefit and chronicled as a city improvement.

We will now take the reader to that grand old structure,

FORT MARION.

Standing at the northeastern end of the town, its site was most excellently chosen for the protection of the city in those days, being that its guns command the whole harbor and inlet from the sea, as also the whole peninsula, to the south, north, and west, upon which St. Augustine is built. It is considered a fine specimen of military architecture, having

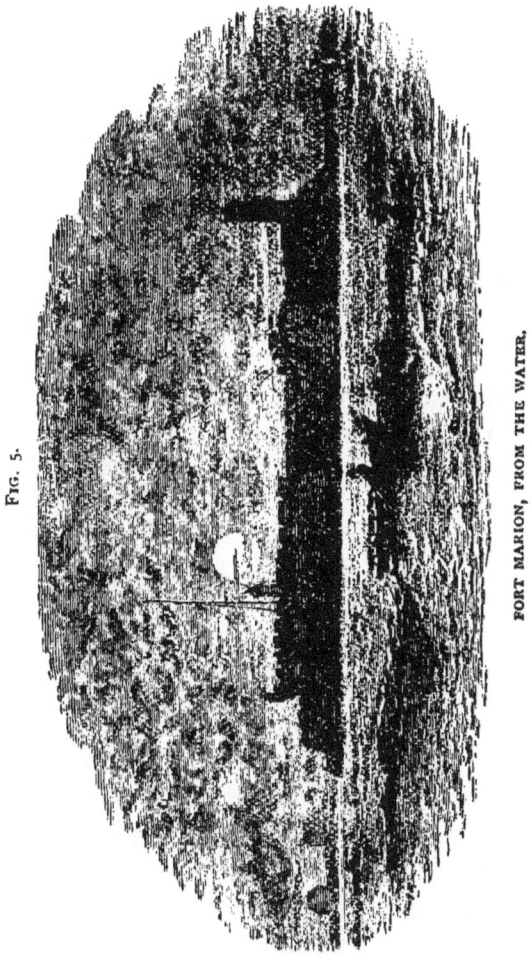

Fig. 5.

FORT MARION, FROM THE WATER.

been constructed on the principles laid down by the famous engineer Vauban.

The walls are twenty-one feet high, with bastions at each corner; the whole structure being in the form of a trapezium, and inclosing an area about sixty yards square. It was begun in 1696 and completed in 1756, being the oldest fortification in the United States. Its first name was "San Juan de Pinos," afterwards changed to "San Marco," and upon the change of flags in 1821 to its present name. In 1879, a petition was sent to Congress to change the name of the old fort to "San Marco," which sounds much more romantic than "Marion;" but this was refused; the reason being that all our forts are named after some great general, and they could make no exception in this case. The fort is built of coquina. The Appalachian Indians were employed upon it for more than sixty years, and to their efforts are probably due the immense labor in the construction of the ditch, the ramparts, the glacis, and the approaches. It undoubtedly required many hundred persons for many years to procure and cut the stone from the quarries of Anastasia Island. During the works of extension and repairs effected by Monteano, previous to the siege by Oglethorpe, he employed upon it one hundred and forty Mexican convicts. It is hard to say how much money it took to build the fort; 'tis said that the King of Spain, in one of his letters to the Governor of St. Augustine, had written that "it almost cost its weight in gold, and that a few such forts would ruin his kingdom."

The fort occupies about four acres of ground, and mounts one hundred guns, requiring a garrison of one thousand men; although larger numbers have, on several occasions, been stationed within its walls. The main entrance was by a drawbridge.* Over the doorway of the entrance is sculp-

---

* Now removed, a stationary one taking its place.

ST. AUGUSTINE. 41

tured, on a block of stone, the Spanish coat of arms, surmounted by the globe and cross, with a Maltese cross and lamb beneath.

Immediately under the arms is this inscription:

REYNANDO EN ESPANA EL SENN DON FERNANDO SEXTO Y SIENDO GOVR Y CAPN DE ESA CD SAN AUGN DE LA FLORIDA Y SUS PROVA EL MARISCAL DE CAMPO DN ALONSO FERNDO HERADA ASI CONCLUIO ESTE CASTILLO EL AN OD 1756 DRIENDO LAS OBRAS EL CAP. INGNRO DN PEDRO DE BROZAS Y GARAY.

TRANSLATION.

Don Ferdinand the VI, being King of Spain, and the Field Marshal Don Alonzo Fernando Hereda, being Governor and Captain General of this place, St. Augustine of Florida, and its province, this Fort was finished in the year 1756. The works were directed by the Captain Engineer, Don Pedro de Brozas y Garay.

On entering you find yourself in the court or parade-ground, one hundred feet square. Inside there are twenty-seven casemates, thirty-five feet long and eighteen feet wide. In former times, during the Indian wars, and in cases of attack by sea, the citizens would flock to this stronghold, and take up their abode in these bomb-proofs. The casemate in front of the sally-port has on each side, as you enter it, a niche that was used for holy water vessels, and at the end is an altar; above the altar is a niche, where was at one time an image of some saint or martyr of the early Church. This was the chapel where service was held. In another bomb-proof is a raised platform; this is supposed to have been the judgment hall, where court-martial was held. In a neighboring casemate is an opening, which was cut for the purpose of discovering an underground passage, which was supposed to connect the

Cathedral and the fort. Under the northeast bastion we find a dark, gloomy dungeon, twenty feet long, six feet wide, and nearly five feet high, where not a ray of light can penetrate. This was once built up, and cut off from all communication with the rest of the fort.

In 1836 the terreplein of the northwest bastion fell in, revealing a dark and dismal dungeon. We have heard from the lips of a reliable person, still a resident of St. Augustine, and who was present at the time of the above accident to the fort, of the following facts: " I stood upon the edge and looked down into this dungeon, and there saw the complete skeleton of a human being, lying at full length, apparently on its back; the arms were extended from the body and the skeleton fingers were wide open; there appeared to be a gold ring upon one of the fingers. Encircling the wrists were iron bands, attached to which were chains fastened to a hasp in the coquina wall, near the entrance to the dungeon."

The military engineer having charge of the repairs of the fort and sea-wall, descended into this dungeon, when his curiosity was excited by the discovery, to the northeast, of a broad stone, differing greatly in dimensions and appearance from those of which the wall was built. He noticed, moreover, that the cement which held this stone in its place differed in composition and appeared to be more recent. On the removal of this stone, the present dark and dismal dungeon was disclosed. On entering with lights there were found at the west end, two iron cages suspended from hasps in the wall. One of the cages had partially fallen down from rust and decay, and human bones lay scattered on the floor. The other remained in its position, holding a pile of human bones. The latter cage and contents may be seen in the Smithsonian Institute at Washington.

This stone was removed by the assistance of Mr. John Capo (now deceased), an honest old harbor pilot and mason; we have his statement, made personally to us, confirming the finding of the two cages containing the skeletons, as presented in this sketch.

From a lecture delivered at the fort by J. Hume Simons, M.D., and afterward published in the *Florida Press*, we quote:

"The broken cage, with all the bones, except those which I hold in my hand, were buried in the sand-mound to the north of the fort. I recognize these as portions of the tibia and fibula (or leg bones) of a female."*

The following letter and item we quote from *Edwards's Guide of East Florida*:

"The story of the finding of iron cages inclosing human skeletons must lose its horrible interest when the following letter is read. It is an answer to one of mine of inquiry on the subject."

SMITHSONIAN INSTITUTE.
JOHN L. EDWARDS, JACKSONVILLE, FLORIDA.

SIR: In reply to your letter of July 20th, we have to say that no objects such as those said to have been found in the dungeon of the old fort at St. Augustine have ever been received by us, although we are aware that the impression is otherwise. Truly yours, etc.,

JOSEPH HENRY,
Secretary Smithsonian Institute.

The following we quote from Dewhurst's excellent *History of St. Augustine*, which is undoubtedly the true story of the cages and skeletons.

---

* Whitney's Pathfinder.

"At the time the Americans took possession of the fort, they found the last casemate, fronting on the court, on the east side, filled with the coquina floor of the terreplein, which had fallen in, as the timbers supporting it had rotted. Naturally this half-filled casemate had become the place of deposit for all rubbish accumulated upon any part of the works. In the course of repairs, the rubbish was cleared out of the casemate, and the entrance into the adjoining cell exposed. Entering this cell, and examining the masonry for anticipated repairs, the engineer in charge, said to be Lieutenant Tuttle, U. S. A., discovered a newness of appearance about a small portion of the masonry of the north wall. Under his instruction a mason cut out this newer stonework, and found that the small arch under which those who now enter the 'dungeon' crawl, had been walled up. . . . . Near the entrance were the remains of a fire, the ashes and bits of pine wood burned off toward the centre of the pile in which they had been consumed. Upon the side of the cell was a rusty staple, with about three links of chain attached thereto. Near the wall on the west side of the cell were a few bones. Finding these very rotten, and crumbling to pieces under his touch, the engineer spread his handkerchief upon the floor, and brushed very gently the few fragments of bones into it. These were shown to the surgeon then stationed at the post, who said they might be human bones, but were so badly crumbled and decayed he could not determine definitely. Nothing else was found in the cell.*

"The iron cages which have been described as a part of the

---

* The finding of any bones is denied by Major W. H. Benham, U. S. A., on the authority of a Mr. Ridgely, Lieutenant Tuttle's overseer. Major Benham took charge of the work upon the fort in January, 1839.

fixtures of this terrible dungeon, and which, it has been said, contained human bones, appear upon the testimony of old inhabitants, to have been found outside the City Gates entirely empty. . . . The cages are described as having had much the shape of a coffin; and the tradition is that a human being had been placed in each, the solid bands of iron riveted about his body, and after life had been extinguished by the horrible torture of starvation, cages and corpses had been buried in the 'scrub,' then covering the ground north of the gates.

"Doubtless these cages were used for the punishment of criminals condemned for some heinous crime; but whether they were introduced by the Spanish or English is unknown."

You have now perused Dewhurst's and Whitney's cage stories. The following has been related by an old citizen, who distinctly remembers that when a child, of from eleven to thirteen years old, there was a tree situated just inside and close to the City Gates, from which was suspended an iron cage; 'twas just high enough for a man to kneel or lie in. This cage contained a man, and suspended above him, just beyond his reach, was a glass of water and a piece of bread, to make the pangs of hunger, from which he suffered, more keen. At the expiration of a few days, his tortures had made him a maniac, and his shrieks, that pierced the air, were something horrible. The person who related the tale is ninety-one years old, which makes this event to have happened about eighty years ago, during Spanish rule in St. Augustine.

The southwest casemate near the well is the one from

which Coa-cou-che, the distinguished Seminole chieftain, made his notable escape in the first Seminole war. This Indian, also called " Wild Cat," was the youngest son of Philip, a great chief among the Seminoles. He was a man of great courage, of an adventurous disposition and savage nature, lacking the intellectual abilities of Osceola, but possessing great influence among his nation. Like most of the young chiefs he was bitterly opposed to the execution of the treaty signed by the older chiefs, by which the Seminoles agreed to remove west of the Mississippi. At an interview immediately before the breaking out of hostilities, Colonel Harney observed to him that unless the Seminoles removed according to the treaty the whites would exterminate them. To this Coa-cou-che replied that Iste-chatte (the Indian) did not understand that word. The Great Spirit, he knew, might exterminate them, but the pale-faces could not, else, why had they not done it before? During the war the young chief was captured and placed under guard in Fort Marion. It is reported that he was first confined in one of the close cells, and in order to be removed to a casemate, which had an embrasure through which he had planned to escape, he complained of the dampness in the cell and feigned sickness. There were at that time quite a number of Indians confined in the fort, and unless they showed themselves querulous and dangerous they were allowed the freedom of the court during the day, and confined at night in the several casemates. It is probable that Coa-cou-che chose the casemate in the southwest bastion, from which to make his escape, because of a platform which is in the casemate. This platform is raised some five feet from the floor and built of masonry, directly under the embrasure through which he escaped. This opening had been constructed high up in the outer wall of the casemate, to admit light and air. It is thirteen feet above the floor, and eight feet above the platform, which had probably been constructed for the convenience of the judges, who doubtless used this casemate for a judgment-room. The aperture is about two feet high by nine inches wide, and some eighteen feet above the level of the ground, at the foot of the wall within the moat. It is said that as he took his airing upon the terreplein, the evening before his escape, Coa-cou-che lingered longer than usual, gazing far out into the west as the sun went down, probably thinking that ere another sunset he would be beyond the limit of his farthest vision, enjoying the freedom of his native forests.

That night he squeezed his body, said to have been attenuated by voluntary abstinence from food, through the embrasure in the wall, and silently dropped into the moat at the foot of the bastion. The moat was dry, and the station of every guard well known to the Indian, so that escape was no longer difficult. Coa-cou-che immediately joined his nation, but was afterwards captured and sent West. He was recalled by General Worth, and used to secure the submission of his tribe. General Worth declared to him, that if his people were not at Tampa on a certain day, he would hang from the yard of the vessel on which he had returned and was then confined. This message he was ordered to send to his people by Indian runners, furnished by the General. He was directed to deliver to the messengers twenty twigs, one for each day, and to make it known to his people that when the last twig in the hands of the messengers was broken, so would the cords which bound his life be snapped asunder, unless they were all at the General's camp, prepared to depart to the reservation provided for them at the West. The struggle in the mind of Coa-cou-che was severe, but his love for life was strong. He sent by the messengers his entreaties that his people should appear at the time and place designated, and take up their abode in the prairies of the West. Desiring to impress upon his people that this was the will of the Great Spirit, with consummate policy he directed the messengers to relate to them this,—Coa-cou-che's dream :*

"The day and manner of my death are given out, so that whatever I may encounter I fear nothing. The spirits of the Seminoles protect me, and the spirit of my twin sister, who died many years ago, watches over me; when I am laid in the earth I shall go to live with her. She died suddenly. I was out hunting, and when seated by my campfire alone, I heard a strange voice,—a voice that told me to go to her. The camp was some distance off, but I took my wife and started. The night was dark and gloomy; the wolves howled about me. I went from hammock to hammock; sounds came oftener to my ear. I thought she was speaking to me. At daylight I reached the camp, but she was dead. I sat down alone, under the long gray moss of the trees, when I heard strange sounds again. I felt myself moving, and went along into a new country, where all was bright and beautiful. I saw clear water, ponds, rivers and prairies, upon which the sun never set. All was green; the grass grew high, and the deer stood in the midst looking at me. I then saw a small white cloud approaching, and when just before me, out of

---

* Dewhurst's St. Augustine.

it came my twin-sister, dressed in white, and covered with bright silver ornaments. Her long black hair, which I had often braided, fell down upon her back; she clasped me around the neck, and said, 'Coa-cou-che! Coa-cou-che!' I shook with fear. I knew her voice, but could not speak. With one hand she gave me a string of white beads, in the other she held a cup sparkling with pure water; as I drank she sang the peace song of the Seminoles, and danced around me; she had silver bells around her feet, which made a loud sweet noise. Taking from her bosom something she laid it before me, when a bright blaze streamed above us; she took me by the hand and said, 'All is peace.' I wanted to ask for others, but she shook her head, stepped into the cloud, and was gone. All was silent. I felt myself sinking until I reached the ground, where I met my brother Chilka."*

Coa-cou-che's appeal was successful. The messengers returned with the whole remnant of the tribe, three days before the expiration of the time. They all embarked, and took up their residence on the prairies, "where the sun never sets and the grass grows high." It was not a field in which Coa-cou-che could distinguish himself, and from this time his name was never heard, except in connection with his past exploits in Florida.

We will now continue our way through the fort. Ascending a broad stairway of two flights, we reach the top or parapet of the fort, from which can be obtained a superb view of the channel and ocean beyond. On this battlement was formerly mounted heavy guns. On the corner of each bastion there was a circular tower; one of these has recently

---

* Sprague's History of the Seminole War.

fallen. On the northern portion of the parapet stood a wooden building, now removed, in which the Indians were confined. These Indians, of the Comanche, Cheyenne, Arapahoe, and Kiowa tribes, who having been selected as among the worst specimens of the wild, cruel savages of the far West, were brought here in May, 1875, from Fort Sill; among them were several noted chiefs. They came in charge of Captain R. H. Pratt, through whose kind treatment, combined with the aid of several charitable ladies, what were when they came here the most savage of their kind, left here in 1878, thoroughly civilized, and many of them able to read and write. The letter which we quote from *Edwards's Guide of East Florida* explains what became of them.

OFFICE OF ASSISTANT QUARTERMASTER,
ST. AUGUSTINE, FLORIDA, September 27th, 1880.
MR. JOHN L. EDWARDS, JACKSONVILLE, FLA.

SIR: The commanding officer has directed me to acknowledge receipt of your note of the 21st instant, and to say in answer thereto that "Medicine Water" and all other Indians at one time confined in Fort Marion, were released by order of the War Department in May, 1878, and turned over to the Interior Department, by which the older ones were sent to Fort Sill, Indian Territory. The younger ones were sent to the "Hampton Normal Institute," Hampton, Virginia, to be educated and taught different trades, which proved to be a very successful experiment. All but seven of the Indians outlived their confinement, and left here in perfect health.

Very respectfully,
JAMES R. MCAULIFF,
2d Lieut. 5th Art'y, Post Adjutant.

The fort sustained a heavy bombardment from the batteries erected on Anastasia Island, by General Oglethorpe, in 1740, but received no injury beyond a few scars on its sea-front, the marks of which are yet visible. When Sir Francis Drake made his attack on the town in 1586, the present site of the fort was covered with a wooden entrenchment, and known by the name of Fort St. John. It was perfectly deserted when Drake approached. Fourteen brass pieces were found mounted on the platforms. An iron-bound chest, containing about £2000, which was intended for payment to the men who garrisoned the fort, was taken by Drake. At this period the town was built of wood, one-half of which was burned by Drake.

FIG. 6.

FORT MARION AT ST. AUGUSTINE, FLORIDA.

In 1665, when Captain Davis, the English pirate, plundered St. Augustine, the fort was constructed of wood, octagonal in shape. 1702 seems to have been the time when the name of St. Mark's was applied to the fort.

History says, that on the arrival of Menendez, in 1565, he immediately constructed a wooden fort, no doubt on the present site. The moat is protected from the sea by a stanch battery, about fifteen feet wide and ten feet high at low tide, which forms a fine promenade, connected with the

SEA WALL,

Which is the next object of interest. This was originally a Spanish structure, the first wall having been built in 1690, extending to the Plaza; but was rebuilt in 1837, and was six years in building, and cost one hundred thousand dollars. It extends from the fort on the Matanzas River to the United States Barracks south, and is about one mile in length. It is ten feet above low-water mark, seven feet at the base, and three feet wide on the top, capped with granite. It forms a fine promenade, just wide enough for two persons to walk abreast, and is a favorite resort for lovers or those who are sentimentally inclined. Near the Plaza and the Barracks the wall is recessed, and forms a basin, where the fishermen bring in their boats, and also for a protection to boats during gales.

ANASTASIA ISLAND,

Which has been mentioned quite a number of times during the recital, is well worthy to have a conspicuous place in the history of St. Augustine, having been more than once the scene of bloodshed and strife. The island is the natural breakwater of St. Augustine, is eighteen miles long and averages about half a mile in width.

In 1586, Sir Francis Drake disembarked at the north end of the island, crossed the harbor, and pillaged the town. General Oglethorpe, in 1740, disembarked at the point opposite Fort Marion. Here he threw up a sand battery, of which a trace remains at the present day. In 1760, there existed on the northeast point of the island a coquina battery, which the encroachment of the sea has entirely destroyed. " The old Spanish lighthouse stood on the northeast side of the island; on Sunday, June 20th, 1880, a storm washed it away, the water having undermined it, and nothing but the ruins of this interesting old landmark remain. When the old lighthouse was built, we have been unable to discover. Under Governor Grant it was raised by a timber construction, and had a cannon planted on it, which was fired as soon as the flag was hoisted to notify the inhabitants and pilots that a vessel was approaching. It had two flag-staffs, one to the north and one to the south, on either of which the flag was hoisted as the vessel was approaching from the north or south. It is possible that the old lighthouse was constructed in 1693, with the proceeds of $6000 appropriated by the Council of the Indies for building a tower as a lookout. The Spaniards kept a detachment of troops stationed there, and the town and adjoining chapel were inclosed with a high and thick stone wall, pierced with loopholes, and having a salient angle to protect the gate."*

About one hundred yards from the ruin of the old, stands the new lighthouse, a noble structure and one of the finest on the Atlantic coast. 'Tis worth a visit to the island to see this splendid building; it is one hundred and sixty-four feet high; its cost was over one hundred thousand dollars, of which the lantern alone cost sixteen thousand. It was erected in 1873. A short distance south are the famous coquina quarries, of which the fort, city gates, and ancient houses are built. The stranger upon first seeing the coquina thinks 'tis artificially formed; 'tis formed over the whole island, by the action of the sea-water on the sand and shells. 'Tis now but seldom used for building purposes, as it is inclined to

---

* Dewhurst's St. Augustine.

54   BLOOMFIELD'S HISTORICAL GUIDE.

hold moisture. 'Tis an excellent stone for foundation and is utilized for that purpose. Anastasia Island on the east is bounded by the Atlantic Ocean, west by Matanzas River, which flows south about eighteen miles and empties into the ocean. The inlet at Matanzas, by which name the southern

FIG. 7.

FORT MATANZAS.

end of the island is known, has still standing the ruins of the structure known as Fort Matanzas. From all accounts, the same was built by the Spaniards directly after the bombardment of Oglethorpe. We quote the following from

Romans's *Florida:* "Twenty miles south of St. Augustine is the lookout, or Fort of Matanzas, on a marshy island, commanding the entrance of Matanzas, which lies opposite to it. This fort is to be seen at about the distance of five leagues. It is of very little strength, nor need it be otherwise, as there is scarce eight feet of water on this bar at the best of times. The Spaniards kept a lieutenant in command here; the English a sergeant." Matanzas is very sparsely settled; in the season there is one hotel open. 'Tis a favorite place for those who enjoy fishing, as this sport is carried on most successfully there. With a fair wind and tide, Matanzas can be reached from St. Augustine in about three hours.

ORANGE GROVES, ROSE GARDENS, ETC.

St. Augustine has a number of very fine groves, in which are cultivated numerous kinds of tropical fruits, such as figs, Japan plums, bananas, dates, pomegranates, guava, lime, lemon, grape fruit, and many others. The finest orange grove is that of Dr. Anderson, who has about fifteen hundred fine bearing trees; this grove is situated on King Street; the entrance is on the right-hand side going towards the depot. From this there is a communicating gate leading to the fine grove belonging to Mrs. Ball. Though not having so many trees, 'tis very much admired by visitors, on account of the grounds, which are beautifully laid out, a promenade through the grand orange arches being very enjoyable, while a stroll through "Lover's Lane" to "Proposing Point" should be made by all followers of the god Cupid. We venture to remark, that the romance of these beautiful surroundings has brought gladness to the hearts of many a fair maiden and gentle swain.

St. Augustine is famous for its beautiful roses. The rose garden of Mrs. Reynolds is situated just in the rear of the Colored Home on Bronson Street. Cut flowers of all kinds can be obtained there at all times. The flower-gardens of Mr. H. H. Williams are very attractively situated on the Shell Road. Mr. Williams is an excellent florist, and shows great skill and taste in arranging bouquets. About half a mile north of this are the grounds of Mr. Hildreth, where an excellent assortment of Florida grasses can be seen; to reach these places a lovely ride of about twenty minutes can be taken. The famous rose tree of Mr. Olivero can be seen at his place on St. George Street near the City Gates. The tree is fifteen feet high, and twenty-one inches in circumference. There are numerous other places where beautiful flowers are cultivated; in fact nearly every private garden can boast of its beautiful plants.

NEW ST. AUGUSTINE

Is situated west of the San Sebastian River. It has a number of neat cottages, among the most pretentious of which is the elegant residence of Mr. G. Van Dorn. Mr. Bevan is also commodiously quartered in his neat cottage, surrounded by a lovely orange grove, which contains other rare and tropical fruits. New St. Augustine is having a boom, and we predict for it a bright future.

RAVENSWOOD.

The visitor having left the depot, passes over the causeway and bridge which lead to St. Augustine.

From the bridge looking north, on the left, will be observed the recently erected dwelling of John F. Whitney, Esq., the proprietor of the new projected settlement of Ravenswood.

This is the pioneer residence located upon this tract of over one thousand acres. From its close proximity to St. Augustine, and its sloping, dry, and healthful position, it promises soon to become a favorite location for Northerners desirous of building-sites and orange groves in the immediate neighborhood of the ancient city.

THE YACHT CLUB

Is one of *the* institutions of St. Augustine, the majority of its membership being composed of wealthy Northerners who spend their winters here. The club-house is pleasantly situated on the bay diagonally opposite the Plaza. The interior is richly furnished, and nothing is left undone that would promote the comfort of the members and their guests. The gala days held here every March, under the auspices of the club, are considered the great event of the season.

Nothing can be more picturesque or fairy-like than their illumination night, when every yacht on the bay is gayly lit with many-colored lanterns. At the receptions of the Yacht Club are represented some of America's fairest daughters and bravest sons, and they are undoubtedly the most *recherche* events of the season.

HANDSOME WINTER RESIDENCES.

Among the many advancements St. Augustine has made in the last ten years is the number of elegant winter residences that have been built, of which the old town has every reason to be proud. On St. George Street, near St. Francis, stands the lovely cottage of Mr. J. L. Wilson, of Framingham, Mass. On the corner of St. George and Bridge streets is the winter residence of Mr. R. D. Bronson, of New York. The residence of Mr. A. J. Alexander, of Kentucky, stands on the northeast corner of St. George and Bridge streets; directly opposite are the fine grounds and residence of Mr. J. P. Howard, of New York; on the same side of the street, about half a square north, can be seen the residence of Holmes Ammidown, Esq., of New York, whose grounds are a marvel of loveliness, and greatly admired by all. On the corner of King and St. George streets is the winter residence of Colonel Tyler. The profusion of rare plants, and especially the fine specimen of the date, render this garden a very attractive spot. On St. George Street, north of the Plaza, the first fine building that greets the eye is the elegant and massive structure of the Right Reverend Bishop Moore, Bishop of Florida; this is undoubtedly the most solid piece of modern architecture in the city. On the east side of St. George, between Cuna and St. Hypolita streets, is the beautiful villa of George Lorillard, Esq., of New York; 'tis quite an ornament to the city. Outside the City Gates, on the west side, is the fine residence of H. P. Kingsland, Esq., of New York; this residence has a fine orange grove attached to it. Coming from the depot, on King Street, directly under where the pride of India trees spread their branches, is the commodious residence of Mr. Gilbert. Immediately opposite is Dr. A. Anderson's residence, who is also the fortunate possessor of the finest orange grove in the city. The entrance to Mrs. Ball's residence is on Tolomato Street, and is one of the finest constructed houses in the State. On the bay facing the Sea-wall at the corner of Treasury Street, is the handsome coquina residence of Mr. D. Edgar, of New York. South of the Plaza stands the residence of Mr. Aspinwall, of New York, and just below is the residence of Miss Worth, daughter of General Worth, of Mexican War fame.

BATHING, YACHTING, FISHING, AND HUNTING.

In summer, a short sail to the beach, and you can enjoy the most delightful kind of surf bathing. In winter, at the bath-house on the bay, sea bathing can be enjoyed, either hot or cold, a luxury with which no other place in Florida can accommodate you. The yachting facilities are unsurpassed, and many points of interest can thus be visited. Among them is a trip to North Beach, or Point Quartell, as it was formerly called, where shells and sea-beans can be picked up quite plentifully after a heavy gale. Then a trip to the South Beach or Bird's Island, or a visit to Fish's Island, a lovely spot, covered with fine oaks and orange arches, a delightful place for a picnic. Sail-boats can be hired by the hour or day. The steam yacht Maggie also plies regularly between the North and South beaches. The captains of the various boats are all reliable and experienced sailors, and no fear need be entertained as to their ability to manage their boats. The fishing-grounds around St. Augustine are too numerous to itemize. You can enjoy various kinds of fishing here,—bass, drum, sheepshead, shark, catfish, etc. Good hunting can be enjoyed a few miles out of town, game of all kinds being abundant. Generally it is necessary to have a guide on these expeditions. Several good guides can be obtained in St. Augustine. St. Augustine is also noted for its fine salt-water oysters, clams, stone-crabs, and green turtles.

COUNTRY DRIVES.

There are some very fine drives in and about the city, among which are the following:

1. Magnolia Grove.
2. Red House Branch.

3. Hildreth's Farm.
4. Gibbs's Farm.
5. Century Oak.
6. Ponce de Leon Spring.
7. Hanson Grove.
8. King's Road.
9. Bridge of Sighs.
10. Long Swamp.

All within five miles of the city. Any driver can direct you to these places.

HOTELS AND BOARDING-HOUSES.

St. Augustine Hotel, $4 per day, accommodates 300.
Florida House, $4 per day, accommodates 225.
Magnolia Hotel, $4 per day, accommodates 250.

BOARDING-HOUSES.

The following are private houses, whose terms you can better obtain on application in person or by postal communication.

Miss Hazeltine, Mrs. J. V. Hernandez, Colonel Tyler, Mrs. Winslow, Mrs. De Medicis, Mrs. Nelligan, Mrs. Frazier, Mrs. Edwards, Mr. George Greeno, Mrs. Foster, and Mrs. Byrnes; besides which there are two restaurants, and numerous rooms and cottages, that can be rented by day, week, month, or season.

HISTORY OF THE MINORCANS.

The following interesting article I quote from Dewhurst's *History of St. Augustine:*

"The proclamation of Governor Grant, and the accounts which had gone abroad of the advantages of the province, and the liberal policy adopted by the British in the treatment of colonists, induced some wealthy planters from the Carolinas to remove to Florida, and several noblemen of England also solicited grants of land in the province. Among the noblemen who secured grants of land in Florida were Lords Hawke, Egmont, Grenville and Hillsborough, Sir William Duncan and Dennys Rolle, the father of Lord Rolle. Sir William Duncan was a partner with Dr. Turnbull in importing a large number of Europeans for the cultivation of their lands south of St. Augustine, on the Halifax River. The persons whom these two gentlemen then induced to come to Florida are the ancestors of a large majority of the resident population of St. Augustine at the present day. In the early accounts of the place I am satisfied that gross injustice was done to these people in a reckless condemnation of the whole community. I have myself heard their descendants unreasonably censured and their characters severely criticised. These unfavorable opinions were doubtless generated by the unfortunate position in which these immigrants found themselves. Friendless in a strange land, speaking a different language from the remainder of the inhabitants, and of a different religious belief, it was but natural that they should mingle but little with the English residents, especially after they had experienced such unjust treatment at the hands of one of the most influential of the principal men in the colony. The reader will understand the position of these Minorcans and Greeks, and the feelings they must have entertained toward the great men of the colony after reading Romans's account of the hardships they were forced to undergo, and the difficulty they had in breaking their onerous contract. Romans says: 'The situation of the town or settlement made by Dr. Turnbull is called New Smyrna, from the place of the doctor's lady's nativity. About fifteen hundred people, men, women, and children, were deluded away from their native country, where they lived at home in the plentiful cornfields and vineyards of Greece and Italy, to this place, where, instead of plenty, they found want in the last degree; instead of promised fields a dreary wilderness; instead of a grateful, fertile soil, a barren, arid sand, and in addition to their misery were obliged to indent themselves, their wives and children, for many years, to a man who had the most sanguine expectations of transplanting bashawship from the Levant. The better to effect his purpose he granted them a pitiful portion of land for ten years upon the plan of the feudal system. This being improved and just rendered fit for cultivation, at the end of that term it again reverted to the original grantor, and the grantee may, if he chooses, begin a new state of vassalage for ten years more. Many were denied even such grants as these, and were obliged to work at tasks in the field. Their provisions were, at the best of times, only a quart of maize per day, and two ounces of pork per week. This might have sufficed with the help of fish, which abounded in this lagoon; but they were denied the liberty of fishing, and, lest they should not labor enough, inhuman taskmasters were set over them, and, instead of allowing each family to do with their homely fare as they pleased, they were forced to join altogether in one mess, and at the beat of a vile drum to come to one common copper, from whence their hominy was ladled out to them. Even this coarse and scanty meal was, through careless management, rendered still more coarse, and through the knavery of a providetor and the pilferings of a hungry cook, still more scanty. Masters of vessels were forewarned from giving any of them a piece of bread or meat. Imagine to yourself an African—one of a class of men whose hearts are generally callous against the softer feelings—melted with the wants of these wretches, giving them a piece of venison, of which he caught what he pleased, and for this charitable act disgraced, and in course of time used so severely that the unusual servitude soon released him to a happier state. Again, behold a man obliged to whip his own wife for pilfering bread to relieve his helpless family; then think of a time when the small allowance was reduced to half, and see some brave, generous seamen charitably sharing their own allowance with some of these wretches, the merciful tars suffering abuse for their generosity, and the miserable objects of their ill-timed pity undergoing bodily punishment for satisfying the cravings of a long-disappointed appetite, and you may form some judgment of the manner in which New Smyrna was settled. Before I leave this subject I will relate the insurrection to which those unhappy people at New Smyrna were obliged to have recourse, and which the great ones styled rebellion.

"'In the year 1769, at a time when the unparalleled severities of their taskmasters, particularly one Cutter (who had been made a justice of the peace, with no other view than to enable him to execute his barbarities on a larger extent and with greater appearance of authority), had drove wretches to despair, they resolved to escape to Havana. To execute this they broke into the provision stores and seized on some craft lying in the harbor, but were prevented from taking others by the care of the masters. Destitute of any man fit for the important post of leader, their proceedings were all confused, and an Italian of very bad principles, but of so much note that he had formerly been admitted to the overseer's table, assumed a kind of command, they thought themselves secure where they were, and this occasioned a delay till a detachment of the Ninth Regiment had time to arrive, to whom they submitted, except one boatful, which escaped to the Florida Keys, and were taken up by a Providence man. Many were the victims destined to punishment; as I was one of the grand jury, which sat fifteen days on this business, I had an opportunity of canvassing it well, but the accusations were of so small account that we found only five bills; one of these was against a man for maiming the abovesaid Cutter, whom it seems they had pitched upon as the principal object of their resentment, and curtailed his ear and two of his fingers; another for shooting a cow, which, being a capital crime in England, the law making it such was here extended to this province; the others were against the leader, and two more for the burglary committed on the provision store. The distress of the sufferers touched us so that we almost unanimously wished for some happy circumstances that might justify our rejecting all the bills, excepting that against the chief, who was a villain. One man was brought before us three or four times, and, at last, was joined in one accusation with the person who maimed Cutter; yet, no evidence of weight appearing against him, I had an opportunity to remark, by the appearance of some faces in court, that he had been marked, and that the grand jury disappointed the expectations of more than one great man.

Governor Grant pardoned two, and a third was obliged to be the executioner of the remaining two. On this occasion I saw one of the most moving scenes I ever experienced; long and obstinate was the struggle of this man's mind, who repeatedly called out that he chose to die rather than be the executioner of his friends in distress; this not a little perplexed Mr. Woolridge, the sheriff, till at length the entreaties of the victims themselves put an end to the conflict in his breast, by encouraging him how to act. Now we beheld a man thus compelled to mount the ladder, take leave of his friends in the most moving manner, kissing them the moment before he committed them to an ignominious death. Cutter some time after died a lingering death, having experienced besides his wounds the terrors of a coward in power overtaken by vengeance.'

"The original agreement made with the immigrants before leaving the Mediterranean, was much more favorable to them than Romans described it. At the end of three years each head of a family was to have fifty acres of land and twenty-five for each child of his family. This contract was not adhered to on the part of the proprietors, and it was not until, by the authority of the courts, they had secured their freedom from the exactions imposed upon them that any disposition was shown to deed them lands in severalty. After the suppression of this attempt to escape, these people continued to cultivate the lands as before, and large crops of indigo were produced by their labor. Meantime the hardships and injustice practiced against them continued, until in 1776, nine years from their landing in Florida, their number had been reduced by sickness, exposure, and cruel treatment from fourteen hundred to six hundred. At that time it happened that some gentlemen visiting New Smyrna from St. Augustine were heard to remark that if these people knew their rights they never would submit to such treatment, and that the governor ought to protect them. This remark was noted by an intelligent boy, who told it to his mother, upon whom it made such an impression that she could not cease to think and plan how, in some way, their condition might be represented to the governor. Finally, she decided to call a council of the leading men among her people. They assembled soon after in the night, and devised a plan of reaching the governor. Three of the most resolute and competent of their number were selected to make the attempt to reach St. Augustine and lay before the governor a report of their condition.

"In order to account for their absence they asked to be given a long task, or an extra amount of work to be done in a specified time, and if they should complete the work in advance, the intervening time should be their own to go down the coast and catch turtle. This was granted them as a special favor. Having finished their task by the assistance of their friends so as to have several days at their disposal, the three brave men set out along the beach for St. Augustine. The names of these men, most worthy of remembrance, were Pellicier, Llambias, and Genopley. Starting at night, they reached and swam Matanzas Inlet the next morning, and arrived at St. Augustine by sundown of the same day. After inquiry they decided to make a statement of their case to Mr. Young, the attorney-general of the province. No better man could have been selected to represent the cause of the oppressed. They made known to him their condition, the terms of their original contract, and the mandants of those who settled at Smyrna have replaced these palmetto huts with comfortable cottages, and many among them have acquired considerable wealth, and taken rank among the most respected and successful citizens of the town.

ST. AUGUSTINE IN 1817.

The following are the impressions of an English visitor, in 1817:

"Emerging from the solitudes and shades of the pine forests, we espied the distant, yet distinct, lights of the watch-towers of the fortress of St. Augustine, delightful beacons to my weary pilgrimage. The clock was striking ten as I reached the foot of the drawbridge; the sentinels were passing the *alerto* as I demanded an entrance; having answered the preliminary questions, the drawbridge was slowly lowered. The officer of the guard, having received my name and wishes, sent a communication to the governor, who issued orders for my immediate admission. On opening the gate the guard was ready to receive me, and a file of men, with their officer, escorted me to his Excellency, who expressed his satisfaction at my revisit to Florida. I soon retired to the luxury of repose, and the following morning was greeted as an old acquaintance by the members of this little community. I had arrived at a season of general relaxation, on the eve of the Carnival, which is celebrated with much gayety in all Catholic countries. Masks, dominoes, harlequins, punchinellos, and a great variety of grotesque disguises, on horseback, in cars, gigs, and on foot, paraded the streets with guitars, violins, and other instruments; and in the evenings, the houses were open to receive masks, and balls were given in every direction. I was told that in their better days, when their pay was regularly remitted from the Havana, these amusements were admirably conducted, and the rich dresses exhibited on these occasions were not eclipsed by their more fashionable friends in Cuba; but poverty had lessened their spirit for enjoyment, as well as the means for procuring it; enough, however, remained to amuse an idle spectator, and I entered with alacrity into their diversions. About thirty of the hunting warriors of the Seminoles, with their squaws, had arrived, for the purpose of selling the produce of the chase, consisting of bear, deer, tiger, and other skins, bear's grease, and other trifling articles. This savage race, once the lords of the ascendant, are the most formidable border enemies of the United States. This party had arrived, after a range of six months, for the purpose of sale and barter. After trafficking for their commodities, they were seen at various parts of the town, assembled in small groups, seated upon their haunches, like monkeys, passing around their bottles of aqua-dente (the rum of Cuba), their repeated draughts upon which soon exhausted their contents. They then slept off the effects of intoxication, under the wall, exposed to the influence of the sun. Their appearance was extremely wretched; their skins of a dark, dirty, chocolate color, with long, straight, black hair, over which they had spread a quantity of bear's grease. In their ears, and the cartilages of the nose, were inserted rings of silver and brass, with pendants of various shapes. Their features prominent and harsh, and their eyes had a wild and ferocious expression. A torn blanket, or an ill-fashioned dirty linen jacket, is the general costume of these Indians; a triangular piece of cloth passes around the loins. The women vary in their apparel by merely wearing short petticoats, the original color of which were not distinguishable from the various incrustations of dirt. Some of the young squaws were tolerably agreeable, and if well washed and dressed would not have been uninteresting; but the older squaws wore an air of misery and debasement.

"The garrison is composed of a detachment from the Royal regiment of Cuba, with some black troops, who together form a respectable force. The fort and bastions are built of the same material as the houses of the town, coquina. This marine substance is superior to stone, but being liable to splinter from the effects of bombardment; it receives and imbeds the shot, which adds rather than detracts from its strength and security.

"The houses and the rear of the town are intersected and covered with orange groves; their golden fruit and deep green foliage not only render the air agreeable, but beautify the appearance of this interesting little town; in the centre of which (the square) rises a large structure dedicated to the Catholic religion. At the upper end are the remains of a very considerable house, the former residence of the governor of this settlement; but now, 1817, in a state of dilapidation and decay from age and inattention.

"At the southern extremity of the town stands a large building, formerly a monastery of Carthusian Friars, but now occupied as a barrack for the troops of the garrison. At a little distance are four stacks of chimneys, the sole remains of a beautiful range of barracks, built during the occupancy of the British, from 1763 to 1783. For three years the 29th regiment was stationed there, and in that time they did not lose a single man. The proverbial salubrity of the climate has obtained for St. Augustine the designation of the Montpellier of North America; indeed, such is the general character of the Province of East Florida.

"The governor (Copinger) is about forty-five years of age, of active and vigorous mind, anxious to promote by every means in his power the prosperity of the province confided to his command. His urbanity and other amiable qualities render him accessible to the meanest individual, and justice is sure to follow an appeal to his decision. His military talents are well known, and appreciated by his sovereign; and he now holds, in addition to the government of East Florida, the rank of colonel in the Royal regiment of Cuba.

"The clergy consist of the *padre* (priest of the parish), Father Crosby, a native of Wexford, Ireland; a Franciscan friar, the chaplain to the garrison, and an inferior or curé. The social qualities of the *padre*, and the general tolerance of his feelings, render him an acceptable visitor to all his flock. The judge, treasurer, collector, and notary, are the principal officers of the establishment, besides a number of those devoted solely to the military occupations of the garrison. The whole of this society is extremely courteous to strangers; they form one family, and those little jealousies and animosities, so disgraceful to our small English communities, do not sully their meetings of friendly chit-chat, called as in Spain, *turtulias*. The women are deservedly celebrated for their charms; their lovely black eyes have a vast deal of expression; their complexions are a clear brunette; much attention is paid to the arrangement of their hair; at mass they are always well dressed in black silk *basquinas* (petticoats), with the little *mantilla* (black lace veil) over their heads; the men in their military costumes; good order and temperance are their characteristic virtues;

but the vice of gambling too often profanes their social haunts, from which even the fair sex are not excluded. Two days following our arrival, a ball was given by some of the inhabitants, to which I was invited. The elder couples opened it with minuets, succeeded by the younger couples displaying their handsome light figures in Spanish dances."

ST. AUGUSTINE IN 1843—OLD SPANISH CUSTOMS.*

" At length we emerged upon a shrubby plain, and finally came in sight of this oldest city of the United States, seated among its trees on a sandy swell of land, where it has stood for three hundred years. I was struck with its ancient and homely aspect, even at a distance, and could not help likening it to pictures which I had seen of Dutch towns, though it wanted a wind-mill or two to make the resemblance perfect. We drove into a green square, in the midst of which was a monument erected to commemorate the Spanish constitution of 1812, and thence through the narrow streets of the city to our hotel.

" I have called the streets narrow. In few places are they wide enough to allow two carriages to pass abreast. I was told that they were not originally intended for carriages, and that in the time when the town belonged to Spain, many of them were floored with an artificial stone, composed of shells and mortar, which in this climate takes and keeps the hardness of the rock; and that no other vehicle than a handbarrow was allowed to pass over them. In some places you see remnants of this ancient pavement; but for the most part it has been ground into dust under the wheels of the

---

* Bryant.

carts and carriages introduced by the new inhabitants. The old houses, built of a kind of stone which is seemingly a pure concretion of small shells, overhang the streets with their wooden balconies; and the gardens between the houses are fenced on the side of the street with high walls of stone. Peeping over these walls you see branches of the pomegranate, and of the orange-tree, now fragrant with flowers, and rising yet higher, the leaning boughs of the fig, with its broad luxuriant leaves. Occasionally you pass the ruins of houses, walls of stone with arches and staircases of the same material, which once belonged to stately dwellings. You meet in the streets with men of swarthy complexions and foreign physiognomy, and you hear them speaking to each other in a strange language. You are told that these are the remains of those who inhabited the country under the Spanish dominion, and that the dialect you have heard is that of the island of Minorca. 'Twelve years ago,' said an acquaintance of mine, 'when I first visited St. Augustine, it was a fine old Spanish town. A large proportion of the houses which you now see, roofed like barns, were then flat-roofed; they were all of shell-rock, and these modern wooden buildings were not then erected. That old fort which they are now repairing, to fit it for receiving a garrison, was a sort of ruin, for the outworks had partly fallen, and it stood unoccupied by the military, a venerable monument of the Spanish dominion. But the orange groves were the wealth and ornament of St. Augustine, and their produce maintained the inhabitants in comfort. Orange trees of the size and height of the pear tree, often rising higher than the roofs of the houses, embowered the town in perpetual verdure. They stood so close in the groves that they excluded the sun, and the atmosphere was at all times aromatic with their leaves and fruit; and in spring the fragrance of the flowers was almost oppressive.'

"The old fort of St. Mark, now called Fort Marion—a foolish change of name—is a noble work, frowning over the Matanzas, which flows between St. Augustine and the island of Anastasia; and it is worth making a long journey to see. No record remains of its original construction, but it is supposed to have been erected about a hundred and fifty years since, and the shell-rock of which it is built is dark with time. We saw where it had been struck with cannon-balls, which, instead of splitting the rock, became imbedded and clogged among the loosened fragments of shell. This rock is, therefore, one of the best materials for fortifications in the world. We were taken into the ancient prisons of the fort dungeons, one of which was dimly lighted by a grated window, and another entirely without light; and by the flame of a torch we were shown the half-obliterated inscriptions scrawled on the walls, long ago, by prisoners. But in another corner of the fort we were taken to look at the secret cells, which were discovered a few years since in consequence of the sinking of the earth over a narrow apartment between them. These cells are deep under ground, vaulted overhead, and without windows. In one of them a wooden machine was found, which some supposed might have been a rack, and in the other a quantity of human bones. The doors of these cells had been walled up and concealed with stucco, before the fort passed into the hands of the Americans.

"You cannot be in St. Augustine a day without hearing some of its inhabitants speak of its agreeable climate. During the sixteen days of my residence here, the weather has certainly been as delightful as I could imagine. We have the temperature of early June as June is known in New York. The mornings are sometimes a little sultry; but after two or three hours a fresh breeze comes in from the sea, sweeping through the broad piazzas, and breathing in at the windows. At this season it comes laden with the fragrance of the flowers of the pride of India, and sometimes of the orange tree, and sometimes brings the scent of roses, now in bloom. The nights are gratefully cool; and I have been told by a person who has lived here many years, that there are very few nights in summer when you can sleep without a blanket. An acquaintance of mine, an invalid, who has tried various climates, and has kept up a kind of running fight with death for many years, retreating from country to country as he pursued, declares to me that the winter climate of St. Augustine is to be preferred to that of any part of Europe, even that of Sicily, and that it is better than the climate of the West Indies. He finds it genial and equable, at the same time that it is not enfeebling. The summer heats are prevented from being intense by the sea-breeze, of which I have spoken.

"I have looked over the work of Dr. Forry on the climate of the United States, and have been surprised to see the uniformity of climate which he ascribes to Key West. As appears by the observations he has collected, the seasons at that place glide into each other by the softest gradations; and the heat never, even in midsummer, reaches that extreme which is felt in the higher latitudes of the American continent. The climate of Florida is, in fact, an insular climate; the Atlantic on the east, and the Gulf of Mexico on the west, temper the airs that blow over it, making them

ST. AUGUSTINE.

ner in which they had been treated. Mr. Young promised to present their case to the governor and assured them if their statements could be proved, the governor would at once release them from the indentures by which Turnbull claimed to control them. He advised them to return to New Smyrna and bring to St. Augustine all who wished to leave New Smyrna and the service of Turnbull. 'The envoys returned with the glad tidings that their chains were broken and that protection awaited them. Turnbull was absent, but they feared the overseers, whose cruelty they dreaded. They met in secret and chose for their leader, Mr. Pellicier, who was head carpenter. The women and children with the old men were placed in the centre, and the stoutest men, armed with wooden spears, were placed in front and rear. In this order they set off, like the children of Israel, from a place that had proved an Egypt to them. So secretly had they conducted the transaction, that they proceeded some miles before the overseer discovered that the place was deserted. He rode after the fugitives and overtook them before they reached St Augustine, and used every exertion to persuade them to return, but in vain. On the third day they reached St. Augustine, where provisions were served out to them by order of the governor. Their case was tried before the judges, where they were honestly defended by their friend, the attorney-general. Turnbull could show no cause for detaining them, and their freedom was fully established. Lands were offered them at New Smyrna, but they suspected some trick was on foot to get them into Turnbull's hands, and besides they detested the place where they had suffered so much. Lands were therefore assigned them in the north part of the city, where they have built houses and cultivated gardens to this day. Some by industry have acquired large estates; they at this time form a respectable part of the population of the city.'"

It will be seen by the date of their removal to St. Augustine that the unfavorable comments of Romans and the Englishman, whose letter he quotes, upon the population of the town at the cession to Great Britain, could not have referred to the immigrants who came over under contract with Turnbull. It will also be seen that Williams speaks in very complimentary terms of these people and their descendants. I am pleased to quote from an earlier account a very favorable, and, as I believe, a very just tribute to the worth of these Minorcan and Greek settlers and their children. Forbes, in his sketches, says: "They settled in St. Augustine, where their descendants form a numerous, industrious, and virtuous body of people, distinct alike from the indolent character of the Spaniards, and the rapacious habits of some of the strangers who have visited the city since the exchange of flags. In their duties as small farmers, hunters, fishermen, and other laborious, but useful, occupations, they contribute more to the real stability of society than any other class of people. Generally temperate in their mode of life, and strict in their moral integrity, they do not yield the palm to the denizens of the land of steady habits. Crime is almost unknown among them. Speaking their native tongue, they move about distinguished by a primitive simplicity and purity as remarkable as their speech." Many of the older citizens, now living, remember the palmetto houses which used to stand in the northern part of the town, built by the people who came up from Smyrna. By their frugality and industry the descen-

cooler in summer and warmer in winter. I do not wonder, therefore, that it is so much the resort of invalids; it would be more so if the softness of its atmosphere and the beauty and serenity of its seasons were generally known. Nor should it be supposed that accommodations for persons in delicate health are wanting; they are, in fact, becoming better with every year, as the demand for them increases. Among the acquaintances whom I have made here, I remember many who having come hither for the benefit of their health, are detained for life by the amenity of the climate. 'It seems to me,' said an intelligent gentleman of this class, the other day, 'as if I could not exist out of Florida. When I go to the North, I feel most sensibly the severe extremes of the weather; the climate of Charleston itself appears harsh to me.'

"The negroes of St. Augustine are a good-looking specimen of the race, and have the appearance of being very well treated. You rarely see a negro in ragged clothing, and the colored children, though slaves, are often dressed with great neatness. In the colored people whom I saw in the Catholic church I remarked a more agreeable, open, and gentle physiognomy than I have been accustomed to see in that class.

"Some old customs which the Minorcans brought with them from their native country are still kept up. On the evening before Easter Sunday, about eleven o'clock, I heard the sound of a serenade in the streets. Going out I found a party of young men with instruments of music grouped about the window of one of the dwellings, singing a hymn, in honor of the Virgin, in the Mahonese dialect. They began, as I am told, with tapping on the shutter. An answering knock within had told them that their visit was welcome, and they immediately began the serenade. If no reply had been heard they would have passed on to another dwelling. This hymn is composed of ten stanzas, and is called the *Fromajardis*.

"Sherivarees are parties of idle people, who dress themselves in grotesque masquerade whenever a widow or widower is married. They often parade about the streets and play buffoon tricks for two or three days, haunting the residence of the new-married pair, and disturbing the whole city with noise and riot.

"The Carnival is a scene of masquerading, which was formerly celebrated by the Spanish and Minorcan populations with much taste and gayety; but since the introduction of an American population it has, during the whole winter, been prostituted to cover drunken revels and to pass the basest objects of society into the abodes of respectable people, to the great annoyance of the civil part of the community.

"These and other customs have long since ceased to exist, and many are already forgotten. One of these was 'shooting the Jews,' originally a religious ceremony, but afterwards a diversion. For many years it was the custom to hang effigies at the street corners and upon the Plaza on the evening of Good Friday. When the bells in the cathedral, which are never rung during Good Friday, began on Saturday morning at ten o'clock to ring the Hallelujah, crowds of men in the streets commenced to shoot with guns and pistols at the hanging effigies. This was continued until some unerring marksman severed the cord about the neck of the image, or perhaps it was riddled and shredded by the fusilade."

ST. AUGUSTINE DURING THE CIVIL WAR.

"The naval forces of the United States took possession of St. Augustine in 1862. Batteries had been mounted at the fort, and a small garrison of Confederate troops were in military occupation of the place, but too few in numbers to offer any resistance, and the city was surrendered by the civil authorities upon the demand of Captain Dupont. The Fourth New Hampshire regiment first garrisoned the city. The old fort was brushed up and repaired, the earthworks strengthened, and barracks built on the platform. Occasionally reconnoitring parties of Confederates approached the town, and on one occasion a festive party of officers, who had gone out to Mr. Solana's, near Picolata, to attend a dance, were captured, with their music and ambulance, by Captain Dickinson, celebrated for many daring exploits. It was even believed that this daring partisan had ridden through the city at night in the guise of a Federal cavalry officer. On another occasion the commanding officer of the garrison at St. Augustine was captured, on the road from Jacksonville, by a Confederate picket. . The inhabitants, isolated from all means of obtaining supplies from without the lines, were reduced to great straits. The only condition upon which they were allowed to purchase was the acceptance of an oath of loyalty. Sympathizing strongly with the South they were placed in an unfortunate position, and many doubtless suffered greatly. At one period those of the citizens who had relatives in the Confederate service were ordered to leave the city. Then ensued a scene which beggars description. Men, women, and children were huddled on board a vessel, and, homeless and helpless, were carried along the coast, and disembarked, shelterless, on the banks of the Nassau River, to make their way to food and shelter as best they could—hardships which hardly seemed called for by any military necessity. Many of the young men of the city went into the Confederate service and served through the war with distinction, but many fell victims on the battlefield, in the hospitals, or from exposure to the rigorous climate of Virginia and Tennessee, to which they were unaccustomed.

"To these misfortunes succeeded to all sales and forcible deprivation of property under the most rigorous construction of most rigorous laws. The unsettling of titles and the loss of means have combined to lessen the ability of the people to do more than try to live, without much effort to improve their homes and the appearance of the city."*

THE ST. JOHN'S RIVER.

This magnificent and capacious body of water, characterized for its waywardness by the Indians as "We-la-ka," meaning that "It has its own way"—flows through East Florida, almost due northward, for 400 miles, until Jacksonville is reached. It then runs directly east into the Atlantic Ocean. It seems to be formed by the numerous small streams from the unexplored regions of the Everglades, though its real source is unknown. There are but few streams in the world that present a more tropical appearance along their whole course. We find orange groves —bitter and sweet—dipping their gold-dappled boughs into its tepid waters; on its banks rises the stately magnolia,

---

* Fairbanks's St. Augustine.

in all its pride, steeping the atmosphere in its rich perfume. The waters of this noble stream are of a dark-blue, and slightly brackish in taste, as far up as Lake George.

The banks of the St. John's are the principal attraction to invalids in search of pleasant surroundings. Thousands of visitors are scattered among its towns and villages every winter, while some few bring camp equipages and pitch their tents in the picturesque forests.

The means of access to all points on the river are easy and comfortable.

Mulberry Grove, on the west bank of the river, 12 miles from Jacksonville, is the first landing. There is a beautiful grove here, a very pleasant resort for picnic parties.

Mandarin, Duval County, Florida, 15 miles from Jacksonville, on the east bank; post-office; population, 250. A convent has been recently established here by the Bishop of Florida, and is now inhabited by the Sisters of Mercy. Mrs. Harriet Beecher Stowe resides here; she has a pleasant cottage, surrounded by 40 acres of land, several of which are planted with orange trees.

This was once the scene of a dreadful massacre by the Seminole Indians. Market gardening is extensively engaged in at this point.

Just beyond this place can be seen the wreck of the Federal transport "Maple Leaf," destroyed by a torpedo during the war.

Orange Park, Clay County, Florida, on the west bank of the river, 15 miles from Jacksonville; post-office.

Hibernia, Clay County, Florida, 23 miles from Jacksonville, on the west bank; post-office. A pleasant and convenient resort for invalids.

Magnolia, Clay County, Florida, 28 miles from Jacksonville, on west bank; post-office. This is one of the most pleasant places on the river, having fine hotel accommodations. It is much frequented by Northerners. Near this place, to the northward, is Black Creek, which is navigable for small steamers as far as Middleburg. A pleasant walk of one mile brings you to

Green Cove Springs, Clay County, Florida, 30 miles from Jacksonville, on the west bank; post-office. The principal attraction here is the fine spring, from which the place derives its name. The waters of this spring are strongly impregnated with sulphur, and have a temperature of about 75 degrees, well adapted for rheumatism and dyspepsia. The bathing facilities are well arranged. This place boasts of two fine hotels and a number of boarding-houses.

Florence, formerly *Hogarth's Wharf*, St. John's County, Florida, 35 miles from Jacksonville, on the east bank; post-office and wood landing.

Picolata, St. John's County, Florida, 40 miles from Jacksonville, on the east bank; post-office. This is the site of an ancient Spanish city, with a fine church and monasteries, erected two centuries ago by Franciscan friars. All that remains at this historical point now is a cabin and field grown up with weeds. This was formerly the landing for St. Augustine, having been used as such until the completion of the St. John's Railroad. Opposite Picolata are the remains of Fort Poppa, erected during the Spanish era.

Tocoi, St. John's County, Florida, 49 miles from Jacksonville, on the east bank; post-office. Here connection is made by the St. John's Railroad with St. Augustine, distant 14 miles.

ST. JOHN'S RIVER. 83

Federal Point, Putnam County, Florida, 58 miles from Jacksonville, on the east bank of the river; post-office and wood landing. This place is becoming noted for its choice fruits. Strawberry culture is an important industry.

Orange Mills, Putnam County, Florida, 63 miles from Jacksonville, on the east bank; post-office. Beautiful orange groves here.

Dancey's Landing, one mile further south, has one of the oldest orange groves on the river, the fruit from which is always sought after.

Oak Villa, on the opposite side of the river; post-office and mail-boat landing.

Pilatka, Putnam County, Florida, 75 miles from Jacksonville, on the west bank of the river; population 2500. This is the chief town south of Jacksonville, both in commercial importance and as a health and pleasure-seeking resort. It has ample hotel accommodations. The Putnam House, the Larkin, St. John's, and Carleton are all fine houses, and during the season are overflowing with guests; post and telegraph offices and two weekly papers. The streets are shaded by wild orange trees, some of which are in full fruit and flower at the same time, giving a beautiful appearance to the town. Pilatka was an old military post in the Indian wars, and many buildings now standing are built on the frames or with the timbers of the old quarters, the enginehouse being the old magazine.

San Mateo, Putnam County, Florida, 80 miles from Jacksonville, on the east bank of the river, 80 feet above its level.

Welaka, Putnam County, Florida, 100 miles from Jacksonville, an old town, and having had at one time some commercial importance, as well as a population of 1000. It is situated at the mouth of the Ocklawaha River, and was formerly the terminus of the boats engaged in that trade. There is a hotel at this point and several stores. The adjacent country is well settled up with industrious and enterprising people, who have been quite successful in orange culture and vegetable-growing. The sulphur spring near by is famous for its medicinal virtues.

Norwalk, Putnam County, Florida, 103 miles from Jacksonville, is a new settlement, but a thriving one, in the midst of a fine orange-growing section.

Mount Royal, Putnam County, Florida, 105 miles from Jacksonville, is an old English settlement, and famous in the early history of the country. A sulphur spring, said to possess wonderful curative powers in rheumatic affections, is close by.

Fruitland, Putnam County, Florida, 105 miles from Jacksonville. This point is the landing for a large settlement in the country back of it, which has many advantages of soil, scenery, etc.

Fort Gates, Putnam County, Florida, 106 miles from Jacksonville, on the west bank of the river, was a military post during the Seminole war. Six miles from here is the famous salt springs. Lake Kerr is also near; it is considered one of the finest hunting-grounds near the St. John's, and is a most beautiful sheet of water. Fort Gates has a fine location, with a beautiful view of Lake George.

Georgetown, Putnam County, Florida, 113 miles from Jacksonville, on the east bank of the river, is a shipping-point of some importance for oranges.

Drayton Island, the largest island in the St. John's River, 116 miles from Jacksonville, contains some 1800 acres of good soil, once largely cultivated in cotton and sugar. It was the seat of a powerful tribe of Indians, who had their plantations here. It is now extensively devoted to the production of oranges and early vegetables.

Lake George, 115 miles from Jacksonville. This beautiful sheet of water is about 18 miles in length, and 10 miles in width. This lake has a number of islands in it; the largest is called Drayton Island. The lake is well stocked with fish and water-fowl of every description. Approaching the southern shore, clothed in eternal verdure, the mouth of the river is scarcely distinguishable on account of its diminished width and the blending of forest and stream. Near the mouth the water is very shallow, not exceeding five feet in depth. Efforts have been made towards its improvement by jetties.

Seville, on the east side of Lake George, is a post-office.

Volusia, Volusia County, Florida, 134 miles from Jacksonville, on the east bank of the river; post-office. This is also the site of an ancient Spanish settlement, no vestige of which remains. An immense land grant was afterwards obtained here from the Spanish government by Mr. Dennison Rolles, an English merchant of wealth, who erected a beautiful mansion and established a home for the unfortunate women from the streets of London, with a view to their reformation. Numerous disasters befell the colony, and it was finally broken up.

Emporia is a new town, started in the interior; distance from Volusia about four miles, amidst pine land.

Astor, Orange County, Florida, northern terminus of the St. John's and Lake Eustis Railway, 134 miles from Jacksonville, on the west side of the river.

Manhattan, Orange County, Florida, is a landing on the west side of the river, 136 miles from Jacksonville.

Bluffton, Volusia County, Florida, 140 miles from Jacksonville, on the east side of the river; post-office. South and east of this point are Lake Dexter and Spring Garden Lake, on the east side of which are very rich lands and large orange groves.

Hawkinsville, Orange County, Florida, 160 miles from Jacksonville, on the west side of the river, is a post-office.

De Land Landing, Volusia County, Florida, 162 miles from Jacksonville, on the east side of the river, is a landing. De Land is 5 miles from this river landing. A stage line connects with mail-boats.

Beresford, Volusia County, Florida, 163 miles from Jacksonville, is a post-office, on the east side of Lake Beresford. There are several landings and orange groves on this lake.

Blue Spring, Volusia County, Florida, 168 miles from Jacksonville, is a landing on the east side of the river. Orange City is two miles and a half from this landing. Stages connect with mail-boats.

Sanford, Orange County, Florida, 193 miles from Jacksonville, on the south side of Lake Monroe; a thriving town, with excellent hotel accommodations, and a favorite resort of tourists and invalids.

Mellenville is the site of Fort Mellen, erected during the Indian wars. In the vicinity are several fine orange groves. It possesses hotel and boarding facilities. Its post-office is located at Sanford.

Enterprise, Volusia County, Florida; county seat; situated on the north side of Lake Monroe; 198 miles from Jacksonville. Excellent hotel, and transportation facilities for hunting parties and tourists. One mile from the hotel is the Green Sulphur Springs, the waters of which are transparent and of a delicate green color. Near Enterprise are the residence and extensive orange grove of Fred. de Bary, Esq., the owner of the Merchant Line of Steamers on the St. John's River.

Lake Jessup, 10 miles south of Lake Monroe; Lake Harney, 15 miles southeast of Lake Monroe; Salt Lake, the landing for Titusville, distant 6 miles; and the Indian River. Lake Poinsett, the head of navigation on the upper St. John's, is the landing for Rock Ledge on the Indian River, distant 2½ miles.

OCKLAWAHA RIVER.

This most singular stream, flowing into the St. John's opposite Weldaka, was not fully explored until the year 1867. For over 150 miles it runs parallel with the St. John's from Lake Apopka, which is its source, through Lakes Harris, Eustis, Griffin, etc., and scarcely a house is to be seen along its course after leaving the lakes, but now and then a landing, with its rich freights of cotton, sugar, oranges, etc., the products of the fertile counties of Putnam and Marion. On account of the narrowness of the stream, and the dense foliage on the banks, its navigation is somewhat difficult.

No visitor to Florida should fail to visit Silver Spring, which rises suddenly from the ground, and, after running 9 miles through Silver Run, empties into the Ocklawaha, 100 miles from its mouth. This spring is one of the wonders of this tropical clime; its waters are seventy-five feet or more in depth, and so transparent that the glistening sand on the bottom looks as if but a few inches beneath the surface.

The principal landings on the Ocklawaha are:

Davenport's, 12 miles from St. John's River, east side.
Boyd's, east side, 19 miles from St. John's River.
Cedar, east side, 29 miles from St. John's River.
Fort Brooke, west side, 35 miles from St. John's River; a military station during the Indian War; formerly connected by road across to St. John's River, and was the distributing point for supplies for the army and the western interior.
Orange Creek, west side, 37 miles from St. John's River; landing for Orange Springs; post-office. At this town is one of the largest sulphur springs in the State; in former days, a popular health resort. There are many fine orange groves now in this locality.
Payne's, west side, 49 miles from St. John's River. A treaty with the Indians was consummated here in 1844, Generals Harney, Taylor, and Duval officiating.
Iola, west side, 50 miles from St. John's River; formerly a shipping-point for products of the Orange Lake region; distant 6 miles.
Log, west side, 59 miles from St. John's River; Fort McCoy Settlement.
Eureka, west side, 61 miles from St. John's River; post-office. Near this landing is the famous Cypress Gate of the Ocklawaha River, there being two large cypress trees, making a narrow passage, between which the boats pass.
Sunday Bluff, on the east side, 70 miles from the St. John's River, derives its name from the action of Rev. Mr. Porter, who, in freighting by barges upon this river, would stop at this bluff and hold religious service on Sundays.
Palmetto Landing, on the west side, 80 miles from the St.

John's River; probably derives its name from the dense forest of palmetto trees adjacent.

Durisosa, on the east side, 90 miles from St. John's River.

Graham's Landing, on the east side, 100 miles from St. John's River.

Grahamville, on the east side, 102 miles from St. John's River; post-office.

Silver Spring Run, 108 miles from St. John's River. This is the confluence of the waters of Silver Spring with the Ocklawaha River. No place in Florida is so widely known as this wonderful pool. A river, deep, rapid, and pellucid, flowing impetuously from a great cave in the depth of the fountain-head; it is a sight to call forth at once the admiration and wonder of the most stoical of travellers. The spring is forty-five feet deep and six hundred feet in diameter. The source of this marvellous and unfailing flood is a mystery. Silver Run, which leads to the Ocklawaha River, is 9 miles in length, and is navigated by steamers, which land at the spring, floating on its pellucid tide, with ample room for a fleet. Fish of great size, and often huge alligators, may be seen floating in the depths, apparently oblivious of impending danger.

HALIFAX AND INDIAN RIVERS.

Matanzas, 18 miles south of St. Augustine. This section is considered an excellent hunting and fishing ground. This is noted as the location of the massacre of the Huguenots by the cruel Menendez, the founder of St. Augustine.

New Britain, on the Halifax River, 15 miles from Mosquito Inlet, and Daytona, on the same river, 10 miles from Mosquito Inlet, are flourishing settlements.

Port Orange, 6 miles south of Daytona, on the west bank of the Halifax River, 4 miles north of Mosquito Inlet, possesses many fine orange groves, and is a growing and thriving settlement.

New Smyrna, on the Hillsborough River, near the coast, and 3 miles south of Mosquito Inlet.

Daytona is located 7 miles south of New Britain, on the Halifax River, and 8 miles north of Mosquito Inlet, possesses a good hotel, and boarding-houses, store, post-office, and other facilities.

Titusville, formerly Sand Point, on Indian River, nearly opposite Merritt's Island. This point is the eastern terminus of the Indian River Railroad.

City Point, 15 miles south of Titusville; Georgiana, on Merritt's Island, 35 miles from Titusville, and Eau Gallie, 10 miles south of Georgiana, are the principal settlements on Indian River. This last-named point is the seat of the State Agricultural College.

This section is the sportsman's paradise, abounding in game and fish. No portion of Florida is more inviting to the hunter or angler. The difficulty of transportation, which formerly deterred many from visiting this portion of the State, has been almost entirely removed, and the ever-increasing number of visitors each season is abundant evidence of its varied attractions.

POINTS ON THE ST. JOHN'S,

SHOWING DISTANCES FROM JACKSONVILLE.

Sailing south is termed *going up* the river. Points marked with a star * are on the right going up.

POINTS ON THE ST. JOHN'S.

	MILES.
Arlington,	2
St. Nicholas,	2
Riverside,*	3
Black Point,*	10
Read's Landing,*	13
Mandarin,	15
Orange Park,*	15
Fruit Cove,	19
Hibernia,*	22
New Switzerland,	23
Remington Park,	25
Magnolia,*	28
Green Cove Spring,*	30
Orange Dale,	34
Hogarth's Landing,	38
Picolata,	45
Tocoi,	52
Federal Point,	60
Orange Mills,	64
Cook's Landing,	65
Dancey's Wharf,	66
Russell's Point,	67
Whetstone,*	68
Russell's Landing,	69
Pilatka,*	75
Hart's Orange Grove,	75
Rawlestown,	78
San Mateo,	80
Edgewater,	80
Buffalo Bluff,*	88
Horse Landing,*	94
Smith's Landing,	96
Nashua,	97
Welaka,	100
Ocklawaha River,*	101
Beecher,	101
Orange Point,	102
Norwalk,*	103
Mt. Royal,	106

	MILES.
Fruitlands,	107
Fort Gates,*	107
Georgetown,	111
Racemo,	112
Lake George,	113
Orange Point,	113
Drayton Island,*	114
Salt Springs,*	119
Benella,*	120
Yellow Bluff,*	121
Spring Garden,*	122
Seville,	126
Spring Grove,	126
Lake View,	132
Astor, St. J. & L. E. R.R.,	134
Volusia,	137
Fort Butler,*	138
Manhattan,*	139
Orange Bluff,	140
St. Francis,*	155
Old Town,*	156
Crow's Landing,*	159
Hawkinsville,*	160
Cabbage Bluff,	162
De Land's Landing,	162
Lake Beresford,	166
Blue Spring,	172
Wekiva,	184
Manuel Landing,	185
Shell Bank,	193
Sanford,*	199
Mellenville,*	200
Fort Reid,*	203
Enterprise,	205
Cook's Ferry,	224
Lake Harney,	225
Sallie's Camp,	229
Salt Lake,	270
Indian River,	276

From Astor by St. J. & L. E. R.R., to:

	MILES.
Lake Eustis,	25
Fort Mason,	25
Leesburg,	51

From Sanford by S. F. R.R., to:

Lake Maitland,	23
Orlando,	25

From Enterprise to:

Smyrna,	30
Halifax,	35
Titusville,	50

ON THE OCKLAWAHA.

The following are the points on this stream, giving the distances from Pilatka:

	MILES.
Mouth of Ocklawaha,	26
Davenport Landing,	34
Blue Spring,	54
Cedar Landing,	55
Fort Brook,	61
Orange Spring Landing,	63
Mahlehet Shoals,	73
Orange Lake Landing,	75
Iola,	76
Forty-Foot Bluff,	80
Log Landing,	85
Gillis Creek,	90
Eureka,	94
Sunday Bluff,	96
Pine Island,	97
Palmetto Landing,	102
Gore's Landing,	108
Durisoe's,	114
Grahamsville Landing,	118

94   BLOOMFIELD'S HISTORICAL GUIDE.

	MILES.
Limpkin Bluff,	122
Delk's Bluff,	126½
Silver Spring Run,	127
Silver Spring,	136½
Merreseu's Landing,	146
Lake Ware Landing,	151
Moss's Bluff,	154
Stark Landing,	186
Slighville,	194
Leesburg,	204
Lake Griffin P. O.,	209
Lovell's Landing,	220
Fennetvella,	224
Fort Mason,	230
Pendryville,	233
Yal-aha,	260
Helena,	273
Okeehumkee P. O.,	275

Distances from Jacksonville to:

Savannah,	172
Charleston,	287
Augusta,	172
Columbia,	389
Charlotte,	495
Florence,	389
Richmond, Va.,	748
Washington,	865
Baltimore,	907
Philadelphia,	1005
New York,	1095
Boston,	1322
Nashville,	653
Cincinnati,	837
St. Louis,	1030
Chicago,	1131
Memphis,	885
Louisville,	838

MAX BLOOMFIELD'S CATALOGUE

— OF —

VIEWS OF ST. AUGUSTINE,

ST. JOHN'S AND OCKLAWAHA RIVERS, AND OTHER SECTIONS OF FLORIDA.

UNDOUBTEDLY THE FINEST COLLECTION IN FLORIDA. ONE HUNDRED AND FIFTY INTERESTING SUBJECTS TO PICK FROM.

ONLY 50 CTS. A DOZEN! 50 CTS.!

AND FINER THAN THE VIEWS SOLD ANYWHERE IN THE **WORLD** FOR $1.50.

EXAMINE THE CONTENTS.

ORDERS BY MAIL PROMPTLY ATTENDED TO.

In ordering by mail, always add 10 cents extra for each dozen to pay for postage. Address all orders to MAX BLOOMFIELD, St. Augustine, Florida, next door to the Post-Office.

Parties ordering Views will please give numbers instead of names.

BLOOMFIELD'S CATALOGUE
OF
VIEWS OF ST. AUGUSTINE.
Fort Series.

1. *Full view of Fort Marion from the Sea-wall.*—A splendid view from the south.

2. *Water Battery*, showing furnace shot-house and curves upon which cannon rested.

3. *Water Battery*, with full view of battery, with promenaders.

4. *Ramparts of the fort*, with an excellent view of St. Augustine.

5. *Southwest angle of the fort*, showing its great architectural beauty.

6. *Southwest angle of the fort*, showing the drawbridge.

7. *Interior of Fort Marion.*—*One of the most interesting pictures in the catalogue*, showing the chapel and the entrance to the subterranean dungeon.

8. *Watch Tower, looking seaward.*—There it stands, like a silent sentinel. Who can tell how many brave men have gazed through its loop-holes, with beating hearts, watching the relentless foe?

9. *The Wild Cat Dungeon*, famous for holding within its four walls the bravest and most daring Seminole chief that ever lived, who made one of the most remarkable escapes from prison that was ever known.

10. *Spanish Coat of Arms*, over the doorway of the fort, a translation of which will be found in Bloomfield's *Historical Guide of St. Augustine.*

11. *Lock of the Subterranean Dungeon*, a great curiosity.

12. *Doorway, Fort Marion.*—A fine view, showing how the drawbridge was pulled in when war, with its fiery brand, appeared.

13. *Drawbridge and entrance to fort*, with Anastasia Island in the distance.

14. *Moat Drawbridge*, showing an excellent view of the moat, which contained *water* in the olden time, and was about four feet deeper.

STREETS IN ST. AUGUSTINE.

15. *Hospital Street*, showing the old Spanish house, in the rear of which the famous Spanish *corridors* stand.

16. *St. George Street*, showing the old, old convent, now torn down, the site being occupied by the fine establishment of the publisher of this catalogue.

17. *St. George Street*, showing the old Spanish Treasury walls. The Florida House now occupies the site.

18. *St. George Street*, showing the old Spanish portion.

19. *Treasury Street*, looking east.

20. *Treasury Street*, looking west. The narrowest street in the city, being only seven feet wide.

21. *Charlotte Street*, looking south.

22. *Charlotte Street*, looking north.

23. *Charlotte Street*, from St. Augustine Hotel.

24. *St. Francis Street.*—A very characteristic view, showing the oldest wall now standing, over which leans a date palm tree, which the oldest inhabitants remember to have stood, just as it stands now, when they were children.

OBJECTS OF INTEREST IN ST. AUGUSTINE.

25. *The Spanish Cathedral.*
26. *The Spanish Cathedral* and monument in Plaza.
27. *The Spanish Cathedral* and St. Augustine Hotel.

28. *The Exterior of the Cathedral* strikes the visitor at once with the quaintness of its architecture. It is one of the oldest houses of worship in America.

29. *Interior of Spanish Cathedral.*—A very interesting view, showing this grand old structure in all its antique beauty, a view every visitor should purchase.

30. *First Mass in St. Augustine.*—This view is taken from a large oil painting in the Cathedral. It shows you the first mass celebrated in America, in 1565.

31. *Interior of the Convent.*—The convent is quite an interesting place to visit. You can obtain fine hand-made laces and other rare fancy articles manufactured by the good Sisters.

32. *The Old Slave Market*, facing the Sea-wall, in the Plaza, is one of the most interesting views in the "ancient city."

33. *Spanish Graveyard*, showing some of the oldest tombs in the country.

34. *New Light-house*, showing Anastasia Island.

35. *New Light-house.* Large. This is one of the finest on the Atlantic coast, the light alone costing $16,000. Well worth a visit. You can easily from the light-house reach the Coquina Quarries.

36. *United States Barracks.*

37. *Sea-wall*, looking south.

38. *Sea-wall*, looking north.

Both views give an excellent idea of the water-front.

39. *Old Spanish Light-house.* The ruins of which can still be seen on Anastasia Island, a short distance from the New Light-house.

40. *Pyramids of Major Dade*, in the Post Cemetery, a full account of which is given in Bloomfield's *Guide of St. Augustine.*

41. *Plaza—St. Augustine.*
42. *Plaza—with "Lightning Express,"* or "Florida Cracker."

These views show both monuments, and are very interesting.

43. *An Orange Archway,* at Mrs. Ball's fine orange grove, on Tolomato Street.
44. *Episcopal Church.*
45. *Interior of Episcopal Church.*
46. *Inmates of Colored Home,* showing some of the cooks and chambermaids of George Washington.
47. *A Bird's-eye View from Florida House,* showing a great many objects of interest.
48. *Corridor of Old Spanish House,* situated on Hospital Street, next door to Mrs. Foster's boarding-house; this view gives a good idea of a Spanish house.
49. *Old City Gate,* looking into St. George Street.
50. *Old City Gate,* looking out on Shell Road.
51. *Old City Gate and Fort in the distance.* This old structure creates more ideas, why it stands there, than anything in the city.
52. *Entrance to St. Augustine,* through a lovely live-oak lane, admired by all.
53. *Monument in Plaza,* erected in 1812, "Plaza de la Constitucion."

Indians—who were prisoners here from 1875 to 1878.

54. *Minimic and his Son.*
55. *Howling Wolf.*
56. *Indian Woman.*
57. *Indians in Soldiers' Clothes.*
58. *Indians in Native War Costume.*

OTHER VIEWS IN AND ABOUT ST. AUGUSTINE.

59. *Ball's Carriage Road*, in Mrs. Ball's grove, showing orange arch.

60. *Productions of St. Augustine.* This view shows the only *real* production.

61. *Hunting Slaves at Matanzas*, gives a good idea of how the runaway negro was caught before the war.

62. *Magnolia Grove*, about five miles from St. Augustine, showing the *live oaks* in all their magnificence, draped with Spanish moss.

63. *Picking Oranges*, at Dr. Anderson's grove.

64. *Uncle Jack*—the oldest negro in St. Augustine.

65. *Moonlight on Matanzas River*.

66. *Fort Matanzas*, an old, old relic.

67. *An Hour's Search*, sometimes called "Hunting in Florida," at any rate a *hunt* that is always crowned with success.

68. *Date Tree*, in Dr. Peck's yard, corner of Treasury and St. George streets.

69. *Palmetto Tree*, with Fort Matanzas in the distance.

HOTELS AND PRIVATE BOARDING HOUSES.

70. *St. Augustine Hotel.*
71. *Florida House.*
72. *Magnolia Hotel.*
73. *Sunnyside House.*
74. *Tyler's House.*
75. *Hazeltine House.*
76. *Edwards's House.*
77. *Patterson House.*
78. *De Medicis House.*

79. *Mrs. Hernandez's House.*
80. *Mrs. Foster's House.*

PRIVATE RESIDENCES.

81. *Mr. Ammidown's Residence.*
82. *Dr. Anderson's Residence.*
83. *Mr. Spear's Residence.*
84. *Mrs. Ball's Residence.*
85. *Mr. Lorillard's Villa.*
86. *Presbyterian Parsonage.*

OCKLAWAHA RIVER VIEWS.

87. *Mouth of the Ocklawaha River.*
88. *Near Graham's Landing*, Ocklawaha River.
89. *Swamps on the Ocklawaha River.*
90. *The Long Stretch*, Ocklawaha River.
91. *Palmetto Landing*, Ocklawaha River.
92. *Near Sandy Bluff*, Ocklawaha River.
93. *The Long Beach*, Ocklawaha River.
94. *Wilderness*, Ocklawaha River.
95. *Leaning Tree*, Ocklawaha River.
96. *Devil's Elbow*, Ocklawaha River.
97. *Devil's Punch Bowl*, Ocklawaha River.
98. *Blasted Tree*, Ocklawaha River.
99. *Living Arch*, Ocklawaha River.
100. *Great Cypress Gates*, Ocklawaha River.
101. *Silver Springs*, Ocklawaha River.

These Ocklawaha River views are undoubtedly the finest taken, and every one should have them, for they depict the most wonderful scenery in Florida.

FLORIDA—FRUITS, FLOWERS AND PLANTS.

102. *Orange Tree.*
103. *Cocoanut Tree.*
104. *Banana Blossom.*
105. *Banana Tree with Fruit.*
106. *Date Tree Blossom.*
107. *Date Tree at Mrs. H. B. Stowe's Mandarin.*
108. *Annunciation Lily.*
109. *Spanish Bayonet in Blossom.*
110. *Cherokee Rose.*
111. *Magnolia Blossom.*
112. *Prickly Pear or Cactus.*
113. *Scrub Palmettos.*
114. *Live Oak Draped with Moss.*
115. *Group of Palmetto Trees.*
116. *Pineapples, growing.*

SOUTHERN AND FLORIDA VIEWS.

St. John's River Views.—It is rather difficult to mention them singly, therefore, I can only say, that they are all excellent views, taken from interesting points. I have 12 different subjects.

117. *Mrs. Mitchell's Place*, opposite Jacksonville.
118. *Entrance to Hart's Orange Grove*, opposite Pilatka.
119. *A Tropical Scene*, showing the alligator in his native home.
120. *Fifteenth Amendment*, or the Darkey and his Mule.
121. *Canal*, connecting Halifax River with Mosquito Inlet, cut out of solid coquina rock.
122. *Camping in Florida.*
123. *Cherubs*—Real nigger angels, *a long way after Raphael.*

124. *Florida Lightning Express*, or " The Cracker's Rig."
125. *Mrs. H. B. Stowe's Residence*, at Mandarin, with the Stowe party.
126. *Mrs. H. B. Stowe's Place*, without party.
127. *Bathing Pool, Green Cove Springs.*
128. *Green Cove Springs.*
129. *Bonaventure at Savannah, Georgia.*
130. *Fountains in Park, Savannah, Georgia.*

I have also a fine assortment of Cabinet and Large Mount views for portfolios, at very reasonable rates.

TOURISTS, ATTENTION.

After you have purchased all the views you want, buy a copy of

BLOOMFIELD'S
ILLUSTRATED HISTORICAL GUIDE OF ST. AUGUSTINE
(WITH MAP),

in which all events of interest appertaining to the old town are recorded. Price only 50 cents.

Containing also a Condensed Guide of the St. John's, Ocklawaha, Indian, and Halifax Rivers.

The Map alone is worth the price. For sale by all booksellers and newsdealers in the State, or sent to any address on receipt of price, by   MAX BLOOMFIELD,
ST. AUGUSTINE, FLA.

www.ingramcontent.com/pod-product-compliance
Lightning Source LLC
Chambersburg PA
CBHW020149170426
43199CB00010B/959